NEW JERSEY
BUCKET LIST GUIDE

D1521414

GEORGE B. GILSON

NEW JERSEY BUCKET LIST GUIDE

Embark on 100 Adventures: Discover Hidden Treasures and Popular Destinations to Design Your Ideal Journey.

Inclusive of an interactive map

GEORGE B. GILSON

REFER TO MAPS SECTION TO VIEW THE INTERACTIVE MAP

NEW JERSEY MAP

TOP 100 MUST VISIT PLACES IN
NEW JERSEY USA.

* High Point State Park
*
Delaware Water Gap National
Recreation Area
* Presby Iris Gardens
*
Ramapo Mountain State
Forest (Upper Lot)
* Palisades Interstate Park
* Lake Hopatcong
*
Wallkill River National Wildlife
Refuge
*
Delaware River Scenic Byway
* Buttermilk Falls
*
Thomas Edison National
Historical Park
*
Paterson Great Falls National
Historical Park
* Liberty Science Center
* Kip's Castle Park
*

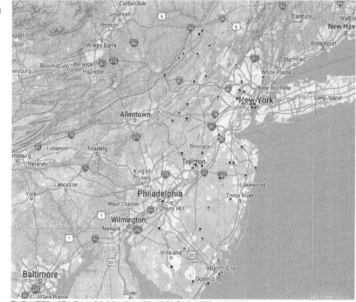

THE INTERACTIVE MAPS OF NEW JERSEY'S TOP ATTRACTIONS

Please consider writing an honest review

3

TABLE OF CONTENTS

9

INTRODUCTION

New Jersey, often called the "Garden State," is a place full of history, natural beauty, and diverse communities. It was one of the original 13 colonies and has played an important role in the story of the United States since its early days. Over the years, New Jersey has grown to nearly 9 million people, thanks to its location between major cities like New York and Philadelphia. This growth has helped make it a bustling state with a strong economy, from its farms to its thriving industries and busy cities.

In this book, we've put together 100 of the best places to visit across New Jersey. Whether you're interested in hiking through scenic parks, exploring charming small towns, or diving into the state's rich history, there's something here for everyone. Each attraction comes with helpful details like why it's worth visiting, what you can do there, and practical tips like GPS coordinates and nearby hotels where you can stay comfortably.

We've also included an interactive map to make planning your trip easier. You can quickly find each destination and see what's nearby, helping you get the most out of your adventure.

So, whether you're a lifelong resident or a first-time visitor, grab this guide, check out the map, and get ready to discover the hidden gems, must-see spots, and unique destinations that make New Jersey special.

Your New Jersey adventure starts now!

New Jersey's Rich History and Culture

New Jersey is a state with a deep and fascinating history, filled with stories of early settlers, battles for independence, and the growth of a diverse and vibrant culture. As one of the original 13 colonies, New Jersey was at the heart of the American Revolution. Towns like Trenton and Princeton were key battle sites where important moments in the fight for independence took place.

Before European settlers arrived, New Jersey was home to the Lenape Native Americans, who lived in harmony with the land for thousands of years. Their legacy can still be seen today in place names, cultural sites, and the state's ongoing respect for nature and community.

In the 1600s, Dutch and Swedish settlers established some of the first European communities in New Jersey, followed by the English who eventually took control. The state grew rapidly due to its fertile land and strategic location between New York and Philadelphia, two major cities that influenced its development.

During the Industrial Revolution, New Jersey became a hub of innovation and industry. Cities like Paterson earned the nickname "Silk City" for its booming silk mills, and the state became known for its manufacturing and transportation networks. Thomas Edison, one of the greatest inventors in history, set up his famous laboratory in Menlo Park, where he invented the lightbulb and many other groundbreaking technologies.

New Jersey's culture is just as rich as its history. The state is a melting pot of cultures, with vibrant communities of people from all over the world. This diversity is reflected in its food, festivals, and traditions. Whether it's enjoying a classic Italian meal in Hoboken, celebrating the Lunar New Year in Fort Lee, or exploring African American history in Atlantic City, New Jersey offers a wealth of cultural experiences.

The state is also known for its contributions to the arts. New Jersey has produced famous musicians like Frank Sinatra and Bruce Springsteen, and its theaters and galleries are alive with creativity. From the bustling art scene in Jersey City to the historic theaters in Newark, the arts are an essential part of New Jersey's identity.

In every corner of New Jersey, from its small towns to its big cities, you can find traces of its rich history and vibrant culture. It's a place where the past and present come together, creating a unique and exciting place to explore and experience.

How to Use This Guide

Welcome to your ultimate guide for exploring the rich history, diverse culture, and natural beauty of New Jersey. This book is your go-to resource, designed to highlight the best places to visit while providing practical tips to make your journey smooth and enjoyable.

This guide offers a detailed overview of New Jersey's top attractions, covering a wide range of destinations including historical sites, natural wonders, cultural events, and more. Each destination is described with key highlights, easy directions, and advice on what to bring to make the most of your visit.

GPS Coordinates and Directions

To help you navigate easily, each destination in this guide comes with precise GPS coordinates. Simply enter these into Google Maps for straightforward navigation. For places that don't have a specific physical address, GPS coordinates ensure you can find your way without any hassle.

Interactive Map

To enhance your travel planning, this guide includes a QR code or link to an interactive map of New Jersey. This digital map shows all the destinations featured in this guide, helping you visualize your journey, plan routes, and discover nearby attractions to make the most out of your trip.

Tips for a Smooth Journey

Preparation: Some areas in New Jersey, especially in more remote or natural settings, may have limited cell signal. It's a good idea to download maps and directions for offline use before starting your journey.

Backup Power: Since you might be exploring for long periods, consider bringing a portable charger or backup battery to keep your devices powered and ready to capture memories.

Seasonal Insights: Each destination includes information on the best times to visit, helping you plan your trip around ideal weather conditions and seasonal events.

Cost Information: This guide provides details on any entry fees, permits, or costs associated with each destination, so you can budget effectively and avoid any surprises.

Making the Most of Your Adventure

This guide isn't just a list of places to visit; it's an invitation to fully experience the unique charm and beauty of New Jersey. Whether you're exploring historic sites, enjoying local cuisine, or taking in the natural landscapes, each destination offers a chance to create lasting memories.

Enjoy all the wonders that New Jersey has to offer!

Landscape of New Jersey

New Jersey is a state with a surprisingly diverse and beautiful landscape. Despite being one of the smallest states in the U.S., it offers a wide range of natural settings, from rolling hills and dense forests to sandy beaches and quiet farmlands.

In the northwest part of the state, you'll find the Kittatinny Mountains, which are part of the Appalachian range. This area is known for its rugged terrain, with hiking trails that offer stunning views, particularly in places like High Point State Park, where you can see all the way to Pennsylvania and New York. The Delaware Water Gap, where the Delaware River cuts through the mountains, is another breathtaking spot, perfect for outdoor activities like hiking, fishing, and kayaking.

Moving to central New Jersey, the landscape shifts to more gentle hills and fertile valleys. This region is often referred to as the "Garden State" because of its rich farmlands. Here, you'll find picturesque farms, orchards, and vineyards that produce fresh fruits, vegetables, and wines. The Raritan River flows through this region, providing scenic riverside trails and opportunities for boating.

The eastern part of New Jersey is known for its famous Jersey Shore. This coastline stretches for about 130 miles along the Atlantic Ocean and features sandy beaches, lively boardwalks, and charming seaside towns. The shore is a popular destination in the summer, with spots like Cape May and Asbury Park attracting visitors who come to enjoy the sun, surf, and local seafood.

In the southern part of the state, you'll encounter the Pine Barrens, a vast area of pine forests, wetlands, and rivers. The Pine Barrens is a unique ecosystem that's home to many rare plants and animals, and it offers a peaceful retreat into nature. This area is also steeped in local legends and history, making it an intriguing place to explore.

Overall, the landscape of New Jersey is much more varied than many people expect. From the mountains in the northwest to the beaches in the east and the forests in the south, New Jersey's natural beauty is something that everyone can enjoy. Whether you're looking for outdoor adventure, relaxing countryside, or a day at the beach, New Jersey has it all.

Climate of New Jersey

New Jersey experiences a varied climate that changes with the seasons, offering a little bit of everything throughout the year. The state is in a temperate zone, which means it has four distinct seasons: spring, summer, fall, and winter.

Spring in New Jersey is a time of renewal, with temperatures gradually warming up after the cold winter months. From March to May, you'll see flowers beginning to bloom, and trees turning green again. The weather can be a bit unpredictable, with some days feeling chilly and others warm, but it's a great time to enjoy outdoor activities as the state comes alive with color.

Summer is when New Jersey really shines, especially along the Jersey Shore. From June to August, temperatures can get quite warm, often reaching the high 80s or low 90s (around 30°C). The beaches become a popular destination as people flock to the coast to cool off in the ocean and enjoy the sun. Inland areas can be hot and humid, but it's also the perfect time for picnics, hiking, and other outdoor fun.

Fall is one of the most beautiful times of the year in New Jersey. From September to November, the temperatures start to drop, making the weather more comfortable. The leaves on the trees change to brilliant shades of red, orange, and yellow, especially in the northern parts of the state. It's a great season for exploring parks and taking scenic drives to enjoy the fall foliage.

Winter in New Jersey can be cold, particularly from December to February. Temperatures often dip below freezing, and snow is common, especially in the northern and western parts of the state. While the coastal areas might see milder winters with less snow, inland areas can experience significant snowfall. Winter sports like skiing and snowboarding are popular in the mountainous regions, while others enjoy cozying up indoors.

Overall, New Jersey's climate offers a little something for everyone, whether you love the warmth of summer or the crisp air of fall. The changing seasons bring different activities and experiences, making it a state that can be enjoyed year-round.

NATURAL WONDERS & OUTDOOR ADVENTURES

High Point State Park

Why You Should Visit: High Point State Park offers stunning views from the highest elevation in New Jersey, where you can see three states. It features hiking trails, lakes, and the High Point Monument, making it a must-visit for nature enthusiasts.

Website:(https://www.state.nj.us/dep/parksandforests/parks /highpoint.html)

Location: 1480 NJ-23, Sussex, NJ 07461, USA.

What to Do: Hiking, swimming, camping, and enjoying scenic views.

Packing List: Hiking boots, water, snacks, and a camera.

Best Time to Visit: Spring to fall.

Fees: $5 per vehicle (NJ residents), $10 (non-residents).

How to Get There: Accessible by car via Route 23.

Closest Town for Accommodation: Stay at High Point Mountain Motel, offering basic amenities and proximity to the park. Website: www.highpointmountainmotel.com Location: 1328 NJ-23, Wantage, NJ 07461, USA.

GPS Coordinates: 41.3205° N, 74.6695° W

Interesting Facts: The High Point Monument was built in 1930 to honor New Jersey's war veterans and offers panoramic views.

Delaware Water Gap National Recreation Area

Why You Should Visit: Delaware Water Gap offers dramatic cliffs, river views, and waterfalls, perfect for outdoor adventures. The area is rich in hiking trails, including part of the Appalachian Trail, and offers excellent opportunities for canoeing and kayaking.

Website: (https://www.nps.gov/dewa/index.htm)

Location: 1978 River Road, Bushkill, PA 18324, USA.

What to Do: Hiking, kayaking, and exploring waterfalls.

Packing List: Waterproof gear, sturdy shoes, and a map.

Best Time to Visit: Spring to fall.

Fees: No entry fee, parking fees at some areas.

How to Get There: Accessible by car via I-80 or Route 206.

Closest Town for Accommodation: Stay at Hotel Fauchère, offering luxury accommodations with historic charm and modern amenities. Website: (https://hotelfauchere.com) Location: 401 Broad St, Milford, PA 18337, USA.

GPS Coordinates: 41.1280° N, 74.8091° W

Interesting Facts: The Delaware Water Gap was formed over 500 million years ago and is a significant natural wonder on the East Coast.

Presby Memorial Iris Gardens

Why You Should Visit: Presby Memorial Iris Gardens is a botanical gem in Montclair, showcasing over 10,000 varieties of irises. The gardens bloom in vibrant colors, creating a stunning display each spring.

Website: (https://www.presbyirisgardens.org)

Location: 474 Upper Mountain Avenue, Montclair, NJ 07043, USA.

What to Do: Stroll through the gardens and take photographs.

Packing List: Camera, sun hat, and water.

Best Time to Visit: Beginning of June or late May.

Fees: Suggested donation of $10.

How to Get There: Accessible by car via Route 23 or Garden State Parkway.

Closest Town for Accommodation: Stay at The MC Hotel, offering stylish accommodations with modern amenities. Website: (https://www.themontclairhotel.com) Location: 690 Bloomfield Ave, Montclair, NJ 07042, USA.

GPS Coordinates: 40.8341° N, 74.2082° W

Interesting Facts: Established in 1927, the gardens are home to one of the largest collections of irises in the United States.

Great Falls of Paterson

Why You Should Visit: Great Falls is a powerful waterfall in Paterson, showcasing industrial history and natural beauty. It's one of the largest waterfalls by volume in the eastern U.S., and a key site in America's early industrialization.

Website: (https://www.nps.gov/pagr/index.htm)

Location: 72 McBride Avenue, Paterson, NJ 07501, USA.
What to Do: View the falls and explore the historic mill ruins.

Packing List: Comfortable shoes and a camera.

Best Time to Visit: Spring and early summer.

Fees: Free entry.

How to Get There: Accessible by car via Route 80.

Closest Town for Accommodation: Stay at Hampton Inn & Suites, offering modern comforts and complimentary breakfast.   Website: (https://www.hilton.com/en/hotels/ewrpthx-hampton-suites-fairfield) Location: 118-124 NJ-23, Fairfield, NJ 07004, USA.

GPS Coordinates: 40.9143° N, 74.1818° W

Interesting Facts: Alexander Hamilton envisioned Paterson as America's first planned industrial city, with the falls as its power source.

Ramapo Mountain State Forest

Why You Should Visit: Ramapo Mountain State Forest offers peaceful lakes, rugged terrain, and diverse trails for outdoor enthusiasts. It's less crowded than other parks, making it ideal for hiking, birdwatching, and mountain biking.

Website www.nj.gov

Location: Hiking Trail Parking Lot, Oakland, NJ 07436

What to Do: Hiking, birdwatching, and fishing.

Packing List: Hiking boots, insect repellent, and snacks.
Best Time to Visit: Fall for foliage, spring for mild weather.

Fees: No entry fee.

How to Get There: Accessible by car via Interstate 287 to Skyline Drive.

Closest Town for Accommodation: Stay at Courtyard by Marriott, offering comfortable rooms and modern amenities.

Website: (https://www.marriott.com/hotels/travel/ewrma-courtyard-mahwah) Location: 140 NJ-17, Mahwah, NJ 07430, USA.

GPS Coordinates: 41.0562° N, 74.2227° W

Interesting Facts: The forest includes Ramapo Lake, a popular spot for fishing and picnicking, and is home to various wildlife species.

Palisades Interstate Park

Why You Should Visit: Palisades Interstate Park offers breathtaking views of the Hudson River and Manhattan skyline from dramatic cliffs. The park is rich in history, with several Revolutionary War sites and scenic hiking trails.

Website: (https://www.njpalisades.org)

Location: Alpine Approach Road, Alpine, NJ 07620, USA.

What to Do: Hiking, picnicking, and visiting historical sites. **Packing List:** Comfortable walking shoes, a camera, and a picnic blanket.

Best Time to Visit: Year-round, with fall offering stunning foliage.

Fees: No entry fee; parking fees apply.

How to Get There: Accessible by car via Palisades Interstate Parkway.

Closest Town for Accommodation: Stay at DoubleTree by Hilton, offering comfortable accommodations with modern amenities. Location: 2117 Route 4 Eastbound, Fort Lee, NJ 07024, USA.

GPS Coordinates: 40.9577° N, 73.9103° W

Interesting Facts: The Palisades cliffs were formed about 200 million years ago and are considered a natural wonder.

Lake Hopatcong

Why You Should Visit: Lake Hopatcong, the largest freshwater lake in New Jersey, is a popular destination for boating, fishing, and swimming. The lake's surrounding parks and trails make it a great spot for family outings and water-based activities.

Website: (https://www.lakehopatcong.org)

Location: Lake Hopatcong, Jefferson, NJ 07849

What to Do: Boating, fishing, and swimming.

Packing List: Swimwear, sunscreen, and fishing gear.

Best Time to Visit: Summer for water activities.

Fees: No entry fee; boat launch fees apply.

How to Get There: Accessible by car via Interstate 80, exit Mount Arlington.

Closest Town for Accommodation: Stay at Holiday Inn Express, offering modern rooms and amenities close to the lake. Location: 176 Howard Blvd, Mt Arlington, NJ 07856, USA.

GPS Coordinates: 40.9456° N, 74.6360° W

Interesting Facts: Lake Hopatcong was a luxury resort destination for wealthy New Yorkers in the early 20th century, and it remains a popular vacation spot today.

Wallkill River National Wildlife Refuge

Why You Should Visit: Wallkill River National Wildlife Refuge is a haven for birdwatchers and nature lovers, offering diverse habitats ranging from wetlands to grasslands. The refuge is perfect for wildlife observation and peaceful nature walks.

Website: (https://www.fws.gov/refuge/wallkill-river)

Location: 1547 County Route 565, Sussex, NJ 07461, USA.

What to Do: Birdwatching, canoeing, and wildlife photography.

Packing List: Binoculars, waterproof boots, and a field guide.

Best Time to Visit: For bird migrations, spring and fall.

Fees: No entry fee.

How to Get There: Accessible by car via Route 23, near the NY border.

Closest Town for Accommodation: Stay at Appalachian Motel, offering basic accommodations near the refuge.

Website: (https://www.appalachianmotel.com) Location: 367 Route 94, Vernon, NJ 07462, USA.

GPS Coordinates: 41.2545° N, 74.4912° W

Interesting Facts: The refuge spans over 5,000 acres and is part of the Atlantic Flyway, a key route for migratory birds.

Delaware River Scenic Byway

Why You Should Visit: The Delaware River Scenic Byway offers a scenic drive along the Delaware River, showcasing historic towns, rolling hills, and beautiful river views. It's perfect for a leisurely road trip through some of New Jersey's most picturesque landscapes.

Website: (https://www.byways.org/explore/byways/10231)

Location: Route 29, starting in Trenton, NJ 08608, USA.

What to Do: Scenic driving, photography, and exploring historic towns.

Packing List: Camera, snacks, and a map.

Best Time to Visit: Fall for vibrant foliage and clear skies.

Fees: No fees for driving the byway.

How to Get There: Accessible by car via Route 29 from Trenton, NJ.

Closest Town for Accommodation: Stay at Lambertville House, offering historic charm and modern amenities. Website: (https://www.lambertvillehouse.com) Location: 32 Bridge St, Lambertville, NJ 08530, USA.

GPS Coordinates: 40.3653° N, 74.9461° W

Interesting Facts: The byway runs through several historic districts and follows the path of the Delaware & Raritan Canal State Park, which was used for transportation in the 19th century.

Buttermilk Falls

Why You Should Visit: Buttermilk Falls is one of New Jersey's tallest waterfalls, offering a tranquil and scenic setting perfect for hiking and nature photography. The falls are nestled in a peaceful forest, making it an ideal spot for a serene outdoor experience.

Website: www.nps.gov

Location: Mountain Road, Layton, NJ 07851, USA.

What to Do: Hiking, nature photography, and waterfall viewing.

Packing List: Sturdy hiking boots, a camera, and water.
Best Time to Visit: Spring for the fullest waterfall flow, or fall for beautiful foliage.

Fees: No entry fee.

How to Get There: Accessible by car via Mountain Road, off of Route 602.

Closest Town for Accommodation: Stay at Pocono Palace Resort, offering romantic accommodations with scenic views, located near the Delaware Water Gap.

Website: www.covepoconoresorts.com Location: 206 Fantasy Road, East Stroudsburg, PA 18302, USA.

GPS Coordinates: 41.1395° N, 74.8886° W

Interesting Facts: Buttermilk Falls is part of the Delaware Water Gap National Recreation Area, and a nearby trail leads to the Appalachian Trail for extended hiking adventures.

HISTORICAL & CULTURAL SITES

Thomas Edison National Historical Park

Why You Should Visit: Thomas Edison National Historical Park preserves the laboratory and home of one of America's greatest inventors. Explore Edison's original workspaces, including the chemistry lab, machine shops, and the library where he worked on innovations like the phonograph and light bulb.

Website: (https://www.nps.gov/edis/index.htm)

Location: 211 Main Street, West Orange, NJ 07052, USA.

What to Do: Tour the historic labs, home, and museum exhibits.

Packing List: Comfortable shoes, a camera, and a notepad for taking notes.

Best Time to Visit: Spring to fall for pleasant weather.

Fees: $15 per person (for ages 16 and older).

How to Get There: Accessible by car via I-280 or by NJ Transit to Orange Station.

Closest Town for Accommodation: Stay at Cambria Hotel West Orange, offering modern amenities close to the park. Location: 12 Rooney Cir, West Orange, NJ 07052, USA.

GPS Coordinates: 40.7860° N, 74.2332° W

Interesting Facts: Edison's laboratory complex was the first of its kind in the world and was where he perfected many of his greatest inventions.

Paterson Great Falls National Historical Park

Why You Should Visit: Paterson, known as the birthplace of the American industrial revolution, is home to the Great Falls, one of the largest waterfalls in the U.S. by volume. The city's rich industrial history is showcased through its mills, historic districts, and the Great Falls National Historical Park. **Website:** (https://www.nps.gov/pagr/index.htm)

Location: 72 McBride Avenue Extension, Paterson, NJ 07501, USA.

What to Do: View the falls, explore historic mills, and visit local museums.

Packing List: Comfortable walking shoes and a camera. **Best Time to Visit:** Spring and early summer when the waterfall is at its fullest. **Fees:** Free entry.

How to Get There: Accessible by car via Route 80, or by NJ Transit to Paterson Station.

Closest Town for Accommodation: Stay at Marriott Saddle Brook, offering modern rooms and amenities near Paterson. Location: 138 New Pehle Ave, Saddle Brook, NJ 07663, USA.

GPS Coordinates: 40.9143° N, 74.1818° W

Interesting Facts: Alexander Hamilton envisioned Paterson as America's first planned industrial city, with the Great Falls as its power source.

Liberty Science Center

Why You Should Visit: Liberty Science Center is a premier science museum featuring interactive exhibits, live demonstrations, and the largest planetarium in the Western Hemisphere. It's a perfect destination for families and science enthusiasts to explore and learn.

Website: (https://lsc.org)

Location: 222 Jersey City Blvd, Jersey City, NJ 07305, USA.

What to Do: Explore hands-on exhibits, watch live science demonstrations, and visit the planetarium.

Packing List: Comfortable shoes and a curiosity for science.

Best Time to Visit: Year-round.

Fees: General admission starts at $29.99 for adults.

How to Get There: Accessible by car via NJ Turnpike, or by PATH train to Exchange Place and then a short shuttle ride.

Closest Town for Accommodation: Stay at Hyatt Regency Jersey City, offering waterfront views and modern amenities near the museum. Location: 2 Exchange Place, Jersey City, NJ 07302, USA.

GPS Coordinates: 40.7081° N, 74.0555° W

Interesting Facts: The Liberty Science Center's planetarium is the largest in the Western Hemisphere, with a 27-meter diameter screen.

Kip's Castle Park

Why You Should Visit: Kip's Castle Park is a stunning 9,000-square-foot medieval-style mansion with spectacular views of the New York City skyline. The castle and its grounds offer a serene retreat, blending history with natural beauty.

Website: (https://www.essexcountyparks.org/parks/kips-castle-park)

Location: 22 Crestmont Road, Verona, NJ 07044, USA.

What to Do: Explore the castle, enjoy the views, and walk the landscaped gardens.

Packing List: Camera, picnic basket, and comfortable shoes.

Best Time to Visit: Spring to fall for the best weather and views.

Fees: Free entry.

How to Get There: Accessible by car via Route 23 or Garden State Parkway.

Closest Town for Accommodation: Stay at The Wilshire Grand Hotel, offering elegant accommodations and complimentary breakfast near Kip's Castle. Website: (https://www.thewilshiregrandhotel.com) Location: 350 Pleasant Valley Way, West Orange, NJ 07052, USA.

GPS Coordinates: 40.8338° N, 74.2295° W

Interesting Facts: The castle was built in 1905 and originally named "Kypsburg" after its original owner, Frederick Kip.

Waterloo Village

Why You Should Visit: Waterloo Village is a restored 19th-century canal town along the Morris Canal, offering a glimpse into New Jersey's industrial past. The village features historic buildings, a working mill, and beautiful surroundings for a peaceful visit.

Website:(https://www.state.nj.us/dep/parksandforests/parks /waterloo.html)

Location: 525 Waterloo Road, Stanhope, NJ 07874, USA.

What to Do: Explore historic buildings, visit the working mill, and walk along the canal.

Packing List: Comfortable shoes, a camera, and a water bottle.

Best Time to Visit: Spring to fall.

Fees: Free entry; fees may apply for special events.

How to Get There: Accessible by car via Interstate 80, exit 25.

Closest Town for Accommodation: Stay at Residence Inn Mt. Olive, offering spacious suites and complimentary breakfast near Waterloo Village. Location: 271 Continental Drive, Stanhope, NJ 07874, USA.

GPS Coordinates: 40.9212° N, 74.7151° W

Interesting Facts: Waterloo Village was a bustling canal town during the 19th century and played a key role in New Jersey's transportation history.

Morris Canal Greenway

Why You Should Visit: The Morris Canal Greenway preserves the historic route of the Morris Canal, which once transported coal and iron across New Jersey. Today, it offers scenic walking and biking trails, connecting various historical and natural sites.

Website: (https://morriscanalgreenway.org)

Location: 525 Waterloo Road, Stanhope, NJ 07874, USA

What to Do: Hiking, biking, and exploring historical sites along the canal.

Packing List: Comfortable walking shoes, a bike (if cycling), and water.

Best Time to Visit: Spring to fall.

Fees: No entry fee.

How to Get There: Accessible by car via various routes depending on the entry point.

Closest Town for Accommodation: Stay at Hyatt House Morristown, offering comfortable suites and amenities near the greenway. Location: 194 Park Ave, Morristown, NJ 07960, USA.

GPS Coordinates: Varies by section; a key segment in Wharton, NJ is at 40.9062° N, 74.5749° W

Interesting Facts: The Morris Canal was an engineering marvel of its time, using a system of locks and inclined planes to move boats over steep terrain.

Morristown National Historical Park

Why You Should Visit: Morristown National Historical Park preserves key Revolutionary War sites, including George Washington's winter headquarters. Explore historical buildings, museums, and beautiful grounds that played a vital role in America's fight for independence.

Website: (https://www.nps.gov/morr/index.htm)

Location: 30 Washington Place, Morristown, NJ 07960, USA.

What to Do: Tour historical sites, visit museums, and walk the park grounds.

Packing List: Comfortable shoes, a camera, and a guidebook for historical context.

Best Time to Visit: Spring to fall for the best weather and full access to the park.

Fees: $7 per person, valid for seven days.

How to Get There: Accessible by car via Interstate 287 or by NJ Transit to Morristown Station.

Closest Town for Accommodation: Stay at The Madison Hotel, offering classic elegance and modern amenities, located near the park. Website: (https://www.themadisonhotel.com) Location: 1 Convent Rd, Morristown, NJ 07960, USA.

GPS Coordinates: 40.7975° N, 74.4771° W

Interesting Facts: During the harsh winter of 1779-1780, George Washington and the Continental Army camped here, enduring the coldest winter of the war.

Montclair Art Museum

Why You Should Visit: Montclair Art Museum is renowned for its American and Native American art collections, housed in a charming Beaux-Arts building. The museum offers a range of exhibits, educational programs, and workshops that engage visitors of all ages.

Website: (https://www.montclairartmuseum.org)

Location: 3 South Mountain Avenue, Montclair, NJ 07042, USA.

What to Do: Explore art exhibits, attend workshops, and participate in educational programs.

Packing List: Comfortable shoes and an interest in art and culture.

Best Time to Visit: Year-round.

Fees: $15 for adults, discounts available for seniors, students, and children.

How to Get There: Accessible by car via Route 23 or by NJ Transit to Montclair Station.

Closest Town for Accommodation: Stay at The George, a stylish boutique hotel offering luxury accommodations in Montclair. Website: (https://www.thegeorgemontclair.com) Location: 37 N Mountain Ave, Montclair, NJ 07042, USA.

GPS Coordinates: 40.8180° N, 74.2214° W

Interesting Facts: The museum was founded in 1914 and was one of the first museums in the U.S. to focus on American art.

New Jersey Performing Arts Center (NJPAC)

Why You Should Visit: NJPAC is one of the largest performing arts centers in the U.S., offering world-class performances ranging from Broadway shows to concerts, dance, and comedy. The center is a cultural hub in New Jersey, attracting renowned artists and diverse audiences.

Website: (https://www.njpac.org)

Location: 1 Center Street, Newark, NJ 07102, USA.

What to Do: Attend performances, enjoy dining, and explore art installations.

Packing List: Dress according to the event; casual for concerts, semi-formal for theater.

Best Time to Visit: Year-round, depending on the event schedule.

Fees: Ticket prices vary by event.

How to Get There: Accessible by car via Interstate 280 or by NJ Transit to Newark Penn Station.

Closest Town for Accommodation: Stay at Hotel Indigo Newark Downtown, offering modern accommodations close to NJPAC. Location: 810 Broad St, Newark, NJ 07102, USA.

GPS Coordinates: 40.7404° N, 74.1676° W

Interesting Facts: Since opening in 1997, NJPAC has hosted over 10 million visitors and continues to be a centerpiece of Newark's cultural scene.

Jersey City Street Art

Why You Should Visit: Jersey City is known for its vibrant street art scene, featuring large-scale murals and graffiti by local and international artists. The street art adds color and character to the city, making it a dynamic destination for art lovers and photographers.

Website: (https://www.jerseycityartscouncil.org/street-art)

Location: Various locations throughout Jersey City, NJ, with a concentration in the Powerhouse Arts District.

What to Do: 888 Newark Avenue, Jersey City, NJ 07306, USA.

Packing List: Comfortable walking shoes, a camera, and a map of mural locations.

Best Time to Visit: Spring to fall for the best weather and vibrant colors.

Fees: Free to explore.

How to Get There: Accessible by car or by PATH train to Grove Street or Exchange Place.

Closest Town for Accommodation: Stay at The Westin Jersey City Newport, which offers opulent lodging with skyline views of Manhattan. Location: 479 Washington Blvd, Jersey City, NJ 07310, USA.

GPS Coordinates: 40.7209° N, 74.0460° W

Interesting Facts: Jersey City's street art scene began to flourish in the early 2000s, and the city now hosts an annual mural festival that attracts artists from around the world.

URBAN ADVENTURES
Ellis Island and Statue of Liberty

Why You Should Visit: Ellis Island and the Statue of Liberty are iconic symbols of freedom and democracy in the U.S. Visitors can explore the history of immigration at Ellis Island and enjoy breathtaking views of the New York City skyline from Liberty Island. **Website:** (https://www.nps.gov/stli/index.htm)

Location: Liberty Island, New York, NY 10004, USA (Access via New Jersey or New York).

What to Do: Tour the Statue of Liberty, visit the Ellis Island Immigration Museum, and take a ferry ride.

Packing List: Comfortable walking shoes, a camera, and water.

Best Time to Visit: Spring to fall

Fees: Ferry tickets: $23.50 for adults (includes access to both islands).

How to Get There: Accessible by ferry from Liberty State Park in New Jersey or Battery Park in New York City. **Closest Town for Accommodation:** Stay at The Westin Jersey City Newport, offering modern luxury and stunning

Manhattan views. Phone: +1 201-626-2900 Location: 479 Washington Blvd, Jersey City, NJ 07310, USA.

GPS Coordinates: 40.6892° N, 74.0445° W

Interesting Facts: Over 12 million immigrants passed through Ellis Island between 1892 and 1954, making it the busiest immigrant inspection station in the U.S.

Hoboken Waterfront

Why You Should Visit: Hoboken Waterfront offers stunning views of the Manhattan skyline, with scenic parks, piers, and walking paths along the Hudson River. It's a vibrant area perfect for outdoor activities, dining, and relaxing by the water.

Website: (https://www.hobokennj.gov/locations/parks-waterfront)

Location: Frank Sinatra Drive, Hoboken, NJ 07030, USA.

What to Do: Walking, cycling, dining, and enjoying river views.

Packing List: Comfortable shoes, a camera, and a light jacket.

Best Time to Visit: Spring to fall.

Fees: Free to explore.

How to Get There: Accessible by car via NJ Turnpike or by PATH train to Hoboken Terminal.

Closest Town for Accommodation: Stay at W Hoboken, offering stylish accommodations with river views and modern amenities. Phone: +1 201-253-2400. Location: 225 River St, Hoboken, NJ 07030, USA.

Interesting Facts: Hoboken is the birthplace of Frank Sinatra, and the waterfront area is named in his honor.

Montclair

Why You Should Visit: Montclair is a charming suburban town known for its vibrant arts scene, historic architecture, and eclectic dining options. The town offers a perfect blend of urban energy and small-town charm, with numerous galleries, theaters, and parks.

Website: (https://www.montclairnjusa.org)

Location: Montclair, NJ 07042, USA.

What to Do: Visit art galleries, dine at local restaurants, and explore historic sites.

Packing List: Comfortable shoes, a camera, and a shopping bag.

Best Time to Visit: Year-round.

Fees: Free to explore; costs vary by activity.

How to Get There: Accessible by car via Garden State Parkway or by NJ Transit to Montclair Station.

Closest Town for Accommodation: Stay at The MC Hotel, offering luxury accommodations in the heart of Montclair. Phone: +1 973-329-6400. Location: 690 Bloomfield Ave, Montclair, NJ 07042, USA.

GPS Coordinates: 40.8259° N, 74.2090° W

Interesting Facts: Montclair is home to the Montclair Art Museum and hosts an annual film festival that draws filmmakers and enthusiasts from around the country.

Newark Museum of Art

Why You Should Visit: The Newark Museum of Art is New Jersey's largest museum, featuring a diverse collection of art, science exhibits, and a planetarium. The museum offers something for everyone, from ancient artifacts to contemporary works, making it a cultural hub in the region.

Website: (https://www.newarkmuseumart.org)

Location: 49 Washington Street, Newark, NJ 07102, USA.
What to Do: Explore art galleries, visit the planetarium, and attend special exhibits.

Packing List: Comfortable shoes and a curiosity for art and science.

Best Time to Visit: Year-round.

Fees: $15 for adults, discounts available for seniors, students, and children.

How to Get There: Accessible by car via Interstate 280 or by NJ Transit to Newark Broad Street Station.

Closest Town for Accommodation: Stay at Hotel Indigo Newark Downtown, offering boutique accommodations with artistic flair. Phone: +1 973-622-0002 Location: 810 Broad St, Newark, NJ 07102, USA.

GPS Coordinates: 40.7437° N, 74.1704° W

Interesting Facts: The museum was founded in 1909 and houses one of the most significant Tibetan art collections in the Western Hemisphere.

Prudential Center

Why You Should Visit: Prudential Center is a premier sports and entertainment venue in Newark, hosting NHL games, concerts, and events throughout the year. It's home to the New Jersey Devils and offers an electrifying atmosphere for sports fans and concertgoers alike.

Website: (https://www.prucenter.com)

Location: 25 Lafayette Street, Newark, NJ 07102, USA.

What to Do: Attend sports events, concerts, and live shows.

Packing List: Event tickets, a jacket, and team merchandise for sports events.

Best Time to Visit: Year-round, depending on event schedules.

Fees: Ticket prices vary by event.

How to Get There: Accessible by car via Interstate 280 or by NJ Transit to Newark Penn Station.

Closest Town for Accommodation: Stay at Courtyard by Marriott Newark Downtown, offering comfortable rooms and easy access to the arena. Phone: +1 973-848-0070 Location: 858 Broad St, Newark, NJ 07102, USA.

GPS Coordinates: 40.7336° N, 74.1703° W

Interesting Facts: The Prudential Center opened in 2007 and is one of the top-ranked venues in the U.S. for both sports and entertainment events.

Morristown Historic Downtown

Why You Should Visit: Morristown's historic downtown is rich in Revolutionary War history, with charming streets lined with 18th-century buildings, boutiques, and cafes. It's a perfect destination for history buffs and those looking to explore a quaint, vibrant downtown.

Website: https://www.morristown-nj.org

Location: Morristown, NJ 07960, USA.

What to Do: Explore historic sites, dine at local restaurants, and shop in unique boutiques.

Packing List: Comfortable shoes, a camera, and a shopping bag.

Best Time to Visit: Spring to fall.

Fees: Free to explore; costs vary by activity.

How to Get There: Accessible by car via Interstate 287 or by NJ Transit to Morristown Station.

Closest Town for Accommodation: Stay at The Madison Hotel, offering classic elegance and modern amenities in a historic setting. Phone: +1 973-285-1800 Location: 1 Convent Rd, Morristown, NJ 07960, USA.

GPS Coordinates: 40.7968° N, 74.4772° W

Interesting Facts: Morristown served as General George Washington's headquarters during the winter of 1779-1780, making it a significant site in American Revolutionary history.

Branch Brook Park

Why You Should Visit: Branch Brook Park in Newark is famous for its stunning cherry blossoms, featuring over 5,000 cherry trees that bloom each spring. The park also offers beautiful walking paths, historic bridges, and serene lakes, making it a perfect spot for a peaceful escape in the city. **Website:** (https://essexcountyparks.org/parks/branch-brook-park)

Location: Park Avenue and Lake Street, Newark, NJ 07104, USA.

What to Do: Enjoy the cherry blossoms, walk the trails, and have a picnic.

Packing List: Comfortable shoes, a camera, and a picnic blanket.

Best Time to Visit: Spring, during the cherry blossom season.

Fees: Free to explore.

How to Get There: Accessible by car via Garden State Parkway or by NJ Transit to Newark Broad Street Station.

Closest Town for Accommodation: Stay at Robert Treat Hotel, offering comfortable accommodations with a historic charm near the park. Phone: +1 973-622-1000. Location: 50 Park Pl, Newark, NJ 07102, USA.

GPS Coordinates: 40.7532° N, 74.1790° W

Interesting Facts: Branch Brook Park was the first county park in the United States, established in 1895, and is now home to the largest collection of cherry blossom trees in the country.

Red Bull Arena

Why You Should Visit: Red Bull Arena in Harrison is the home of the New York Red Bulls soccer team and is considered one of the best soccer-specific stadiums in the United States. The arena offers an exhilarating atmosphere for soccer fans and hosts various events throughout the year.

Website: (https://www.newyorkredbulls.com/redbullarena)

Location: 600 Cape May Street, Harrison, NJ 07029, USA.

What to Do: Attend soccer matches, concerts, and other events.

Packing List: Event tickets, team merchandise, and a jacket for evening games.

Best Time to Visit: March to November, during the soccer season.

Fees: Ticket prices vary by event.

How to Get There: Accessible by car via NJ Turnpike or by PATH train to Harrison Station.

Closest Town for Accommodation: Stay at Element Harrison-Newark, offering modern rooms and eco-friendly

amenities near the arena. Phone: +1 973-484-1500
Location: 399 Somerset St, Harrison, NJ 07029, USA.

GPS Coordinates: 40.7360° N, 74.1502° W

Interesting Facts: Red Bull Arena opened in 2010 and has a seating capacity of 25,000, making it one of the largest soccer-specific stadiums in the U.S.

Jersey City Waterfront

Why You Should Visit: The Jersey City Waterfront offers breathtaking views of the Manhattan skyline, along with parks, piers, and a vibrant dining scene. It's a popular spot for walking, cycling, and enjoying the scenic beauty of the Hudson River.

Website: (https://www.visitnj.org/city/jersey-city)

Location: Jersey City, NJ 07302, USA.

What to Do: Walk or bike along the waterfront, dine at waterfront restaurants, and enjoy the skyline views.

Packing List: Comfortable shoes, a camera, and a light jacket.

Best Time to Visit: Spring to fall for the best weather and outdoor activities.

Fees: Free to explore.

How to Get There: Accessible by car via NJ Turnpike or by PATH train to Exchange Place or Newport Station.

Closest Town for Accommodation: Stay at Hyatt Regency Jersey City, offering luxury waterfront accommodations with stunning views of Manhattan. Phone: +1 201-469-1234 Location: 2 Exchange Pl, Jersey City, NJ 07302, USA.

GPS Coordinates: 40.7178° N, 74.0338° W

Interesting Facts: Jersey City's waterfront is home to Liberty State Park, where visitors can catch ferries to the Statue of Liberty and Ellis Island.

NATURAL WONDERS & OUTDOOR ADVENTURES

Delaware and Raritan Canal State Park

Why You Should Visit: Delaware and Raritan Canal State Park offers a serene escape with its 70-mile-long canal that winds through picturesque landscapes. The park is perfect for outdoor enthusiasts, offering opportunities for hiking, biking, and paddling. You can also explore historical sites along the canal, making it a great spot for both nature lovers and history buffs.

Location: Runs between New Brunswick and Trenton, NJ.

What to Do: Walking, cycling, kayaking, and fishing.

Packing List: Comfortable shoes, water, snacks, a camera.

Best Time to Visit: Spring to fall for the best weather.

Fees: Free entry; fees may apply for activities like kayaking.

How to Get There: Accessible by car via Route 1 or Route 29.

Closest Town for Accommodation: Stay at Hyatt Regency New Brunswick, offering modern rooms and amenities. Phone: +1 732-873-1234

GPS Coordinates: 40.5297° N, 74.4640° W

Interesting Facts: The canal was once a major transportation route in the 19th century, linking Philadelphia and New York.

Grounds for Sculpture

Why You Should Visit: Grounds for Sculpture is an enchanting outdoor sculpture park and museum that spans 42 acres. It features over 270 contemporary sculptures set amidst beautifully landscaped gardens, offering a unique blend of art and nature. Visitors can explore the creative works of renowned artists while enjoying a peaceful and picturesque environment, making it a must-visit for art enthusiasts and families alike.

Website: (https://www.groundsforsculpture.org)

Location: 80 Sculptors Way, Hamilton, NJ 08619, USA.

What to Do: Explore sculptures, walk the gardens, and enjoy a meal at the on-site restaurant.

Packing List: Comfortable walking shoes, a camera.

Best Time to Visit: Spring to fall for the best garden views.

Fees: $20 for adults; discounts for students, seniors, and children.

How to Get There: Accessible by car via Interstate 295 or NJ Turnpike.

Closest Town for Accommodation: Stay at Hilton Garden Inn Hamilton, offering comfortable rooms and an indoor pool. Phone: +1 609-585-6789

GPS Coordinates: 40.2324° N, 74.7137° W

Interesting Facts: The park was founded in 1992 by sculptor Seward Johnson and includes works by renowned artists from around the world.

Edwin B. Forsythe National Wildlife Refuge

Why You Should Visit: Edwin B. Forsythe National Wildlife Refuge protects over 47,000 acres of coastal habitats, making it a crucial sanctuary for migratory birds and other wildlife. Visitors can enjoy peaceful walking trails, scenic drives, and excellent birdwatching opportunities. The refuge offers a tranquil escape into nature, where you can connect with the outdoors and witness the beauty of New Jersey's coastal ecosystems.

Website: (https://www.fws.gov/refuge/edwin-b-forsythe)

Location: 800 Great Creek Road, Galloway, NJ 08205, USA.

What to Do: Birdwatching, photography, and hiking. **Packing List:** Binoculars, a camera, sunscreen, and insect repellent.

Best Time to Visit: Spring or fall

Fees: Free entry.

How to Get There: Accessible by car via Garden State Parkway, exit 48.

Closest Town for Accommodation: Stay at Seaview, A Dolce Hotel, offering elegant accommodations and golf courses nearby. Phone: +1 609-652-1800

GPS Coordinates: 39.4644° N, 74.4450° W

Interesting Facts: The refuge is named after a New Jersey congressman who was an advocate for wildlife conservation.

Round Valley Reservoir

Why You Should Visit: Round Valley Reservoir is known for its deep, clear waters, making it a popular destination for boating, fishing, and scuba diving. The surrounding area offers scenic hiking trails and camping spots, providing a perfect getaway for outdoor enthusiasts. With its pristine waters and tranquil setting, Round Valley Reservoir is a hidden gem for those seeking relaxation and adventure in New Jersey's natural beauty.

Location: 1220 Lebanon-Stanton Road, Lebanon, NJ 08833, USA.

What to Do: Swimming, fishing, hiking, and camping. **Packing List:** Swimwear, fishing gear, hiking boots, and camping supplies.

Best Time to Visit: Summer for water activities; fall for hiking.

Fees: $10 per vehicle for non-residents (summer season).

How to Get There: Accessible by car via Interstate 78. **Closest Town for Accommodation:** Stay at Courtyard by Marriott Lebanon, offering comfortable rooms and modern amenities. Phone: +1 908-236-8500

GPS Coordinates: 40.6191° N, 74.8494° W

Interesting Facts: Round Valley Reservoir is one of the deepest lakes in New Jersey, reaching depths of up to 180 feet.

Mount Tammany

Why You Should Visit: Mount Tammany offers one of the best hikes in New Jersey, with a challenging trail leading to breathtaking views of the Delaware Water Gap. The hike is popular for its panoramic vistas of the Delaware River and surrounding mountains, making it a rewarding experience for those who love outdoor adventures. Whether you're an experienced hiker or a nature enthusiast, Mount Tammany provides a memorable and picturesque escape into nature.

Website: (https://www.nps.gov/dewa/index.htm)

Location: Near Dunnfield Creek Natural Area, Knowlton Township, NJ 07832, USA.

What to Do: Hiking, nature photography, and picnicking. **Packing List:** Sturdy hiking boots, water, snacks, and a camera.

Best Time to Visit: Spring to fall for ideal hiking conditions.

Fees: Free entry.

How to Get There: Accessible by car via Interstate 80, exit 1.

Closest Town for Accommodation: Stay at Pocono Palace Resort, offering romantic suites and lake views near the Delaware Water Gap. Phone: +1 888-963-3048

GPS Coordinates: 40.9708° N, 75.1241° W

Interesting Facts: Mount Tammany is named after a Lenape chief and is part of the Appalachian Mountains.

Rutgers Gardens

Why You Should Visit: Rutgers Gardens is a lush, green oasis offering a variety of themed gardens, walking trails, and a farmers market. As part of Rutgers University, the gardens provide a serene setting for relaxation, education, and exploration. Visitors can enjoy the beauty of seasonal flowers, learn about different plant species, and participate in events that highlight the importance of horticulture and sustainability.

Website: (https://rutgersgardens.rutgers.edu)

Location: 112 Log Cabin Rd, North Brunswick Township, NJ 08902

What to Do: Explore gardens, attend events, and visit the farmers market.

Packing List: Comfortable shoes, a camera, and a reusable bag for market purchases.

Best Time to Visit: Spring or summer.

Fees: Free entry.

How to Get There: Accessible by car via Route 1 or NJ Turnpike, exit 9.

Closest Town for Accommodation: Stay at Hyatt Regency New Brunswick, offering modern accommodations close to Rutgers University. Phone: +1 732-873-1234

GPS Coordinates: 40.4745° N, 74.4375° W

Interesting Facts: The gardens cover over 180 acres and include a bamboo forest, rain garden, and an arboretum.

Pine Barrens

Why You Should Visit: The Pine Barrens is a massive forest in southern New Jersey, covering over a million acres. It's a unique and mysterious place with sandy trails, pine trees, and rare plants. Outdoor lovers can hike, kayak, or camp while exploring this beautiful and wild area. The Pine Barrens is also famous for its ghost towns and the legend of the Jersey Devil, adding a sense of adventure to your visit.

Website: (https://www.nps.gov/pine/index.htm)

Location: Highway Route 72 East, New Lisbon, NJ 08064.

Geographical Coordinates: 39.6232° N, 74.6476° W
What to Do: Hiking, kayaking, camping, and wildlife watching.

Packing List: Sturdy shoes, insect repellent, a map, water.

Best Time to Visit: Spring and fall for mild weather and fewer bugs.

Fees: Free entry; camping fees may apply.

How to Get There: Accessible by car via Garden State Parkway or Route 206.

Closest Town for Accommodation: Stay at The Red Lion Inn & Suites, 175 S White Horse Pike, Hammonton, NJ 08037, USA.

Phone: +1 609-561-5700

Interesting Facts: The Pine Barrens is home to the legendary Jersey Devil, a mythical creature said to roam the forest.

Garden State Parkway Scenic Drive

Why You Should Visit: The Garden State Parkway Scenic Drive is a beautiful way to experience New Jersey's diverse landscapes, from sandy beaches to lush forests. As you drive along the Parkway, you'll pass by charming coastal towns, stunning shorelines, and peaceful parks. It's perfect for a leisurely road trip, where you can stop to enjoy the views, explore local attractions, or simply take in the natural beauty of the Garden State.

Website: (https://www.state.nj.us/turnpike/gs-pkwy.htm)

Location: Entry point at Cape May, NJ 08204, USA. **Geographical Coordinates:** 38.9351° N, 74.9060° W. **What to Do:** Scenic driving, exploring coastal towns, and visiting parks.

Packing List: Map or GPS, snacks, and a camera for capturing scenic views.

Best Time to Visit: Spring and fall for the best scenery and mild weather.

Fees: Tolls apply along the Parkway.

How to Get There: Accessible by car, entering from various points along the New Jersey coast.

Closest Town for Accommodation: Stay at The Reeds at Shelter Haven, 9601 3rd Ave, Stone Harbor, NJ 08247, USA. Phone: +1 609-368-0100

Interesting Facts: The Parkway was opened in 1954 and is known for its picturesque routes along the Jersey Shore, making it one of the most scenic drives in the state.

Spruce Run Recreation Area

Why You Should Visit: Spruce Run Recreation Area is a great spot for outdoor fun, with a large reservoir perfect for swimming, boating, and fishing. The surrounding park offers plenty of space for picnics, camping, and hiking, making it a popular destination for families and outdoor lovers. Whether you're looking to relax by the water or enjoy an active day in nature, Spruce Run has something for everyone.

Website:(https://www.state.nj.us/dep/parksandforests/parks/spruce.html)

Location: 68 Van Syckel's Road, Clinton, NJ 08809, USA.
Geographical Coordinates: 40.6516° N, 74.9394° W.
What to Do: Boating, fishing, swimming, hiking, and camping.

Packing List: Swimwear, fishing gear, picnic supplies, and camping equipment.

Best Time to Visit: Summer for water activities; fall for hiking and camping.

Fees: $10 per vehicle for non-residents (summer season).

How to Get There: Accessible by car via Interstate 78, exit 17.

Closest Town for Accommodation: Stay at Hampton Inn Clinton, 16 Frontage Dr, Clinton, NJ 08809, USA. Phone: +1 908-713-4800

Interesting Facts: Spruce Run is one of New Jersey's first major reservoirs, created in the 1960s to supply water to the surrounding communities.

Hunterdon County Hot Air Balloon Ride

Why You Should Visit: Taking a hot air balloon ride in Hunterdon County is a magical way to see New Jersey from above. As you float over the rolling hills, farms, and rivers, you'll get a peaceful, bird's-eye view of the beautiful countryside. It's a unique and unforgettable experience, perfect for a special occasion or just to enjoy the stunning scenery from a new perspective.

Website: (https://www.njballooning.com)

Location: 176 Airport Road, Pittstown, NJ 08867, USA.

Geographical Coordinates: 40.6365° N, 74.9110° W

What to Do: Hot air ballooning, photography, and enjoying panoramic views.

Packing List: Comfortable clothing, a camera, and sunglasses.

Best Time to Visit: Spring to fall, with calm winds and clear skies.

Fees: Prices vary; typically around $200-300 per person.

How to Get There: Accessible by car via Interstate 78 to Clinton, NJ.

Closest Town for Accommodation: Stay at Holiday Inn Clinton - Bridgewater, 111 W Main St, Clinton, NJ 08809, USA. Phone: +1 908-735-5111

Interesting Facts: Hunterdon County is known for its beautiful rural landscapes, making it one of the top spots for hot air ballooning in New Jersey.

HISTORICAL & CULTURAL SITES

Princeton University

Why You Should Visit: Princeton University is one of the most prestigious universities in the world, known for its beautiful campus, rich history, and academic excellence. Walking through its ivy-covered buildings, you can explore landmarks like Nassau Hall and the Princeton University Art Museum. The campus is not just a place of learning but also a place of stunning architecture and serene gardens.

Website: (https://www.princeton.edu)

Location: Nassau St, Princeton, NJ 08544, USA.

What to Do: Explore the campus, visit the art museum, and stroll through the gardens.

Packing List: Comfortable walking shoes, a camera, and a bottle of water.

Best Time to Visit: Spring or fall

Fees: Free to walk around; some attractions may have fees.

How to Get There: Accessible by car via US-1, or by train to Princeton Station.

Closest Town for Accommodation: Stay at Nassau Inn, offering historic charm with modern comforts in the heart of Princeton. Phone: +1 609-921-7500

GPS Coordinates: 40.3487° N, 74.6599° W

Interesting Facts: Princeton University was founded in 1746 and has produced many notable alumni, including U.S. presidents and Nobel laureates.

Old Barracks Museum

Why You Should Visit: The Old Barracks Museum in Trenton is a historic site that dates back to the French and Indian War. It played a crucial role during the American Revolution as a military hospital and quarters for British and Hessian soldiers. Today, it offers a glimpse into 18th-century military life, with reenactments and exhibits that bring history to life.

Website: (https://www.barracks.org)

Location: 101 Barrack St, Trenton, NJ 08608, USA.

What to Do: Tour the barracks, watch historical reenactments, and view exhibits.

Packing List: Comfortable shoes, a camera, and weather-appropriate clothing.

Best Time to Visit: Year-round; check for special events.

Fees: $10 for adults; discounts for seniors and students.

How to Get There: Accessible by car via Route 1, or by train to Trenton Station.

Closest Town for Accommodation: Stay at Wyndham Garden Trenton, offering modern amenities and close proximity to historic sites. Phone: +1 609-421-4000

GPS Coordinates: 40.2204° N, 74.7693° W

Interesting Facts: The Old Barracks is the only remaining colonial barracks in New Jersey and one of the few left in the United States.

New Jersey State Museum

Why You Should Visit: The New Jersey State Museum in Trenton is a cultural treasure trove that showcases the state's rich history, art, and natural sciences. With exhibits ranging from dinosaur fossils to fine art, the museum offers something for everyone. The planetarium is a highlight, providing educational shows about space and the stars.

Website: (https://www.state.nj.us/state/museum)

Location: 205 West State Street, Trenton, NJ 08608, USA.

What to Do: Explore history exhibits, visit the planetarium, and view art collections.

Packing List: Comfortable shoes and an interest in history and science.

Best Time to Visit: Year-round.

Fees: $5 suggested donation; planetarium shows have a fee.

How to Get There: Accessible by car via Route 1, or by train to Trenton Station.

Closest Town for Accommodation: Stay at Lafayette Park Hotel and Suites, offering comfortable accommodations close to the museum. Phone: +1 609-394-2500

GPS Coordinates: 40.2204° N, 74.7693° W

Interesting Facts: The museum's collection includes over 2 million artifacts, ranging from Native American artifacts to modern art.

Naval Air Station Wildwood Aviation Museum

Why You Should Visit: Naval Air Station Wildwood Aviation Museum is located in a historic World War II hangar and features over 26 aircraft, engines, exhibits, and interactive displays. Visitors can explore the planes up close, learn about aviation history, and even climb into the cockpit of certain aircraft. It's a fantastic experience for aviation enthusiasts and families alike.

Website: (https://www.usnasw.org)

Location: 500 Forrestal Rd, Cape May, NJ 08204, USA.

What to Do: Tour the aircraft, explore exhibits, and enjoy interactive displays.

Packing List: Comfortable shoes, a camera, and sun protection.

Best Time to Visit: Spring to fall.

Fees: $14 for adults; discounts for children and seniors.

How to Get There: Accessible by car via Garden State Parkway, exit 4B.

Closest Town for Accommodation: Stay at Congress Hall in Cape May, offering beachfront accommodations with historic charm. Phone: +1 609-884-8421

GPS Coordinates: 38.9483° N, 74.9080° W

Interesting Facts: The museum is housed in Hangar #1, which was built during World War II and served as a training facility for dive-bomber squadrons.

Allaire Village

Why You Should Visit: Allaire Village is a historic 19th-century iron-making town that has been restored to its former glory. Visitors can explore the blacksmith shop, general store, and other buildings that showcase life during the early 1800s. The village often hosts special events, including craft fairs and reenactments, making it a lively and educational experience for all ages. **Website:** (https://www.allairevillage.org)

Location: 4265 Atlantic Ave, Wall Township, NJ 07727, USA.

What to Do: Explore historic buildings, watch demonstrations, and attend events.

Packing List: Comfortable shoes, a camera, and weather-appropriate clothing.

Best Time to Visit: Spring to fall; check the website for event schedules.

Fees: $5 per person; event fees may vary.

How to Get There: Accessible by car via Garden State Parkway, exit 98.

Closest Town for Accommodation: Stay at Courtyard by Marriott Wall at Monmouth Shores Corporate Park, offering modern amenities close to Allaire Village. Phone: +1 732-919-2780

GPS Coordinates: 40.1534° N, 74.1215° W

Interesting Facts: Allaire Village was once a thriving industrial community known for its iron production, and today it serves as a living history museum.

Sayen House and Gardens

Why You Should Visit: Sayen House and Gardens is a hidden gem in Hamilton, offering beautifully landscaped gardens and a charming historic house. The gardens feature a wide variety of flowers, including stunning azaleas, rhododendrons, and more. It's a perfect place for a peaceful walk, photography, or a relaxing afternoon surrounded by nature.

Website: (https://www.hamiltonnj.com/sayengardens)

Location: 155 Hughes Dr, Hamilton Township, NJ 08690, USA.

What to Do: Explore the gardens, take photos, and enjoy the peaceful surroundings.

Packing List: Comfortable walking shoes, a camera, and a picnic blanket.

Best Time to Visit: Spring and early summer for peak bloom.

Fees: Free entry.

How to Get There: Accessible by car via Route 130 or Interstate 295.

Closest Town for Accommodation: Stay at Hilton Garden Inn Hamilton, offering comfortable rooms and an indoor pool. Phone: +1 609-585-6789

GPS Coordinates: 40.2253° N, 74.6812° W

Interesting Facts: The gardens were established in 1912 by Frederick Sayen, a world traveler who brought back rare and exotic plants from his journeys.

Howell Living History Farm

Why You Should Visit: Howell Living History Farm offers a step back in time to experience farm life as it was in the early 1900s. Visitors can participate in traditional farming activities like plowing, planting, and harvesting. The farm also has animals, a blacksmith shop, and seasonal events that provide an authentic and hands-on experience for all ages.

Website: (https://www.howellfarm.org)

Location: 70 Wooden's Ln, Lambertville, NJ 08530, USA.

What to Do: Participate in farm activities, visit the animals, and explore the grounds.

Packing List: Comfortable clothing, sturdy shoes.

Best Time to Visit: Spring to fall; check for seasonal events.

Fees: Free entry; some activities may have fees.

How to Get There: Accessible by car via Route 29 or Interstate 295.

Closest Town for Accommodation: Stay at Lambertville House, offering boutique accommodations with historic charm in Lambertville. Phone: +1 609-397-0200

GPS Coordinates: 40.3318° N, 74.9119° W

Interesting Facts: The farm dates back to the 1700s and is now a living history museum where visitors can learn about and experience traditional farming techniques used in the past.

Freehold Historic Downtown

Why You Should Visit: Freehold Historic Downtown is a charming area that preserves the rich history of Monmouth County. With its well-preserved 18th and 19th-century buildings, this downtown area is perfect for a leisurely stroll, shopping in unique boutiques, and dining in local restaurants. The town is also home to significant Revolutionary War history, adding an educational twist to your visit.

Website: (https://downtownfreehold.com)

Location: Main St, Freehold, NJ 07728, USA.

What to Do: Walk around historic sites, shop, and dine at local eateries.

Packing List: Comfortable shoes, a camera, and a shopping bag.

Best Time to Visit: Spring to fall for pleasant weather and outdoor events.

Fees: Free to explore; costs vary by activity.

How to Get There: Accessible by car via Route 9 or Route 33.

Closest Town for Accommodation: Stay at American Hotel, offering modern amenities with historic charm in downtown Freehold. Phone: +1 732-431-3220

GPS Coordinates: 40.2600° N, 74.2734° W

Interesting Facts: Freehold was the site of the Battle of Monmouth during the American Revolutionary War, one of the largest battles of the conflict.

Monmouth Battlefield State Park

Why You Should Visit: Monmouth Battlefield State Park is a historic site where one of the largest battles of the American Revolution was fought. The park offers a mix of history and natural beauty, with its rolling hills, orchards, and woodlands. Visitors can explore the battlefield, hike the trails, and learn about the battle through informative exhibits and reenactments.

Website:(https://www.state.nj.us/dep/parksandforests/parks/monbat.html)

Location: 20 NJ-33 Business, Manalapan Township, NJ 07726.

What to Do: Explore historic battlefields, hike trails, and visit the visitor center.

Packing List: Comfortable shoes, a hat, and water.

Best Time to Visit: Spring to fall; summer for reenactments.

Fees: Free entry.

How to Get There: Accessible by car via Route 9 or Route 33.

Closest Town for Accommodation: Stay at Radisson Freehold, offering modern amenities and close proximity to the park. Phone: +1 732-780-3400

GPS Coordinates: 40.2603° N, 74.3242° W

Interesting Facts: The Battle of Monmouth was a key moment in the American Revolution, and the park preserves this important piece of history with its well-maintained grounds and reenactments.

Sterling Hill Mining Museum

Why You Should Visit: This unique museum is built around a former zinc mine and offers visitors a fascinating glimpse into the world of mining. One of the highlights is the fluorescent mineral display, where visitors can walk through glowing tunnels filled with naturally fluorescent minerals. The museum also offers guided tours of the underground mine, showcasing the history and geology of the region.

Address: 30 Plant Street, Ogdensburg, NJ 07439, USA.

What to Do: Take a guided underground mine tour, explore the museum exhibits, and enjoy the fluorescent mineral display.

Packing List: Wear comfortable shoes and light jacket.

Best Time to Visit: Open year-round

Fees: Admission fees apply.

How to Get There: Accessible via Route 23 North, with parking available on-site.

Closest Town for Accommodation: Newton, NJ – Holiday Inn Express & Suites Newton Sparta, offering modern amenities, complimentary breakfast, and easy access to the museum.

Coordinates: 41.0807° N, 74.5958° W

Interesting Facts: The Sterling Hill Mine is one of the oldest mines in the United States and is renowned for its collection of over 350 different mineral species, making it a must-see for geology enthusiasts and curious visitors alike.

URBAN ADVENTURES

Princeton

Why You Should Visit: Princeton is a picturesque town that's home to the prestigious Princeton University. The town blends academic excellence with a charming small-town vibe, offering visitors beautiful historic buildings, lush gardens, and cultural attractions like the Princeton University Art Museum. Walking through Princeton's streets, you'll find a mix of history, culture, and a peaceful atmosphere that makes it a must-visit. **Website:** (https://www.princeton.edu)

Location: Nassau St, Princeton, NJ 08544, USA.

What to Do: Explore Princeton University, visit the art museum, and enjoy local cafes and shops.

Packing List: Comfortable walking shoes, a camera, and a daypack.

Best Time to Visit: Spring and fall.

Fees: Free to explore; some attractions may have entry fees.

How to Get There: Accessible by car via US-1, or by train to Princeton Station.

Closest Town for Accommodation: Stay at Nassau Inn, offering historic charm and modern comforts in downtown Princeton. Phone: +1 609-921-7500

GPS Coordinates: 40.3487° N, 74.6599° W

Interesting Facts: Princeton University was founded in 1746, making it one of the oldest universities in the United States.

New Brunswick

Why You Should Visit: New Brunswick is a lively city known for its cultural diversity, vibrant arts scene, and strong connection to Rutgers University. The city offers a variety of attractions, including theaters, museums, and a bustling downtown filled with restaurants and shops. Whether you're exploring historic sites like the Buccleuch Mansion or enjoying the local culinary scene, New Brunswick has something for everyone.

Website: (https://www.cityofnewbrunswick.org)

Location: New Brunswick, NJ 08901, USA.

What to Do: Visit museums, dine at local restaurants, and explore historic sites.

Packing List: Comfortable shoes, a camera, and a city map.

Best Time to Visit: Year-round; summer is great for outdoor events and festivals.

Fees: Free to explore; costs vary by activity.

How to Get There: Accessible by car via Route 1 or by train to New Brunswick Station.

Closest Town for Accommodation: Stay at The Heldrich Hotel, offering upscale accommodations and easy access to downtown attractions. Phone: +1 732-729-4670

GPS Coordinates: 40.4862° N, 74.4518° W

Interesting Facts: New Brunswick is often called the "Healthcare City" due to its many medical facilities, including the renowned Robert Wood Johnson University Hospital.

Asbury Park

Why You Should Visit: Asbury Park is a vibrant coastal city with a rich musical heritage, famous for its lively boardwalk and arts scene. The town offers a mix of beautiful beaches, historic sites, and a variety of entertainment options, including live music venues like The Stone Pony. Whether you're soaking up the sun on the beach or exploring the eclectic shops and restaurants, Asbury Park provides a perfect blend of relaxation and excitement.

Website: (https://www.apboardwalk.com)

Location: Asbury Park, NJ 07712, USA.

What to Do: Enjoy the beach, visit live music venues, and explore the boardwalk.

Packing List: Beachwear, sunscreen, and a camera.

Best Time to Visit: Summer for beach activities and festivals.

Fees: Free to explore; beach access fees apply during the summer.

How to Get There: Accessible by car via Garden State Parkway, or by train to Asbury Park Station.

Closest Town for Accommodation: Stay at The Asbury Hotel, offering modern accommodations just steps from the boardwalk. Phone: +1 732-774-7100

GPS Coordinates: 40.2204° N, 74.0121° W

Interesting Facts: Asbury Park is known as the birthplace of Bruce Springsteen's music career, with The Stone Pony being a legendary venue in his early days.

Count Basie Center for the Arts

Why You Should Visit: The Count Basie Center for the Arts in Red Bank is a premier performing arts center that hosts a wide range of events, from concerts and comedy shows to Broadway performances. Named after the legendary jazz musician Count Basie, who was born in Red Bank, the center is a cultural hub for both locals and visitors. The beautifully restored theater provides an intimate setting for enjoying top-notch entertainment.

Website: (https://www.thebasie.org)

Location: 99 Monmouth St, Red Bank, NJ 07701, USA.

What to Do: Attend live performances, concerts, and theater shows.

Packing List: Event tickets, a light jacket, and a camera.

Best Time to Visit: Year-round, depending on the event schedule.

Fees: Ticket prices vary by event.

How to Get There: Accessible by car via Garden State Parkway, or by train to Red Bank Station.

Closest Town for Accommodation: Stay at Molly Pitcher Inn, offering elegant accommodations with river views in Red Bank. Phone: +1 732-747-2500

GPS Coordinates: 40.3498° N, 74.0664° W

Interesting Facts: The theater was originally opened in 1926 as a vaudeville house and has since become a cornerstone of the arts in New Jersey.

State Theatre in New Brunswick

Why You Should Visit: The State Theatre in New Brunswick is a historic venue that hosts a variety of performances, including Broadway shows, concerts, and comedy acts. Built in 1921, this beautifully restored theater offers a mix of classic charm and modern amenities, making it a great place to enjoy a night of entertainment. The State Theatre is a key cultural institution in New Brunswick, attracting top performers from around the world. **Website:** (https://www.stnj.org)

Location: 15 Livingston Ave, New Brunswick, NJ 08901, USA.

What to Do: Attend theater productions, concerts, and special events.

Packing List: Event tickets, comfortable clothing, a camera.

Best Time to Visit: Year-round, depending on the show schedule.

Fees: Ticket prices vary by event.

How to Get There: Accessible by car via Route 18, or by train to New Brunswick Station.

Closest Town for Accommodation: Stay at The Heldrich Hotel, offering stylish accommodations just a short walk from the theater. Phone: +1 732-729-4670

GPS Coordinates: 40.4931° N, 74.4456° W

Interesting Facts: The State Theatre was designed by renowned theater architect Thomas W. Lamb and has been a centerpiece of New Brunswick's cultural scene for nearly a century.

Red Bank

Why You Should Visit: Red Bank is a charming riverside town known for its artsy vibe, historic architecture, and vibrant downtown scene. The town is home to unique shops, art galleries, and some of the best restaurants in the area. Red Bank is also a cultural hotspot with venues like the Count Basie Center for the Arts, making it a great place to explore both day and night.

Website: (https://www.redbank.org)

Location: Red Bank, NJ 07701, USA.

What to Do: Shop at boutiques, dine at local restaurants, and enjoy live performances.

Packing List: Comfortable shoes, a camera, and a shopping bag.

Best Time to Visit: Spring or fall

Fees: Free to explore; costs vary by activity.

How to Get There: Accessible by car via Garden State Parkway, or by train to Red Bank Station.

Closest Town for Accommodation: Stay at The Oyster Point Hotel, offering riverside views and modern amenities in Red Bank. Phone: +1 732-530-8200

GPS Coordinates: 40.3471° N, 74.0652° W

Interesting Facts: Red Bank was named after the red soil found along the banks of the Navesink River and has a rich history dating back to the 17th century.

Asbury Park Boardwalk

Why You Should Visit: The Asbury Park Boardwalk is a lively and iconic destination on the Jersey Shore, known for its historic charm and vibrant atmosphere. The boardwalk offers a mix of entertainment, dining, and shopping, all set against the backdrop of beautiful ocean views. Whether you're enjoying a day at the beach, catching a live show, or exploring the unique shops, the Asbury Park Boardwalk is a must-visit for a classic seaside experience. **Website:** (https://www.apboardwalk.com)

Location: Asbury Park, NJ 07712, USA.

What to Do: Stroll the boardwalk, visit shops, dine at restaurants, and enjoy the beach.

Packing List: Beachwear, sunscreen, and a camera.

Best Time to Visit: Summer for beach activities and events.

Fees: Free to explore; beach access fees apply during the summer.

How to Get There: Accessible by car via Garden State Parkway, or by train to Asbury Park Station.

Closest Town for Accommodation: Stay at The Asbury Hotel, offering modern accommodations with a rooftop lounge and close proximity to the boardwalk. Phone: +1 732-774-7100

GPS Coordinates: 40.2204° N, 74.0121° W

Interesting Facts: The Asbury Park Boardwalk was originally built in the late 1800s and has since become a cultural icon, featuring in films, music videos, and album covers.

Silverball Museum Arcade

Why You Should Visit: The Silverball Museum Arcade in Asbury Park is a paradise for pinball and arcade game lovers, featuring a vast collection of vintage machines from the 1950s to the present. This hands-on museum allows you to play all the games, making it a nostalgic and fun experience for visitors of all ages. Whether you're a pinball wizard or just looking for some retro fun, this spot is a must-visit.

Website: (https://silverballmuseum.com/asbury-park)

Location: 1000 Ocean Ave, Asbury Park, NJ 07712, USA.

What to Do: Play vintage pinball machines and classic arcade games.

Packing List: Casual attire, comfortable shoes, and quarters for extra playtime.

Best Time to Visit: Year-round, especially on rainy days or for evening fun.

Fees: $12.50 for one-hour play; various options available.

How to Get There: Accessible by car via Garden State Parkway, or by train to Asbury Park Station.

Closest Town for Accommodation: Stay at The Asbury Hotel, offering easy access to the boardwalk and arcade, with modern rooms and amenities. Phone: +1 732-774-7100

GPS Coordinates: 40.2230° N, 74.0002° W

Interesting Facts: The museum features over 600 games in rotation, making it one of the largest collections of playable pinball and arcade machines in the world.

New Brunswick Culinary Scene

Why You Should Visit: New Brunswick's culinary scene is diverse and vibrant, offering everything from gourmet dining to casual eateries. With its mix of international cuisine, farm-to-table restaurants, and trendy spots, New Brunswick is a food lover's paradise. The city is known for its innovative chefs and a variety of dining options that cater to all tastes and budgets, making it a great destination for a culinary adventure.

Website: (https://www.cityofnewbrunswick.org)

Location: New Brunswick, NJ 08901, USA.

What to Do: Dine at top-rated restaurants, explore local food markets, and try diverse cuisines.

Packing List: An appetite, comfortable shoes, and a list of must-try spots.

Best Time to Visit: Year-round, with outdoor dining in summer and cozy spots in winter.

Fees: Costs vary by restaurant.

How to Get There: Accessible by car via Route 1, or by train to New Brunswick Station.

Closest Town for Accommodation: Stay at The Heldrich Hotel, offering stylish accommodations and easy access to the city's top dining spots. Phone: +1 732-729-4670

GPS Coordinates: 40.4862° N, 74.4518° W

Interesting Facts: New Brunswick is home to several James Beard-nominated chefs and hosts annual food festivals that celebrate the city's culinary diversity.

The Stone Pony in Asbury Park

Why You Should Visit: The Stone Pony is one of the most legendary music venues in the United States, famous for its role in launching the careers of iconic musicians like Bruce Springsteen and Bon Jovi. This intimate venue continues to be a hotspot for live music, hosting a wide range of performances from rock to indie bands. Whether you're a music aficionado or just looking for a fun night out, The Stone Pony offers an unforgettable experience.

Website: (https://www.stoponyonline.com)

Location: 913 Ocean Ave, Asbury Park, NJ 07712, USA.

What to Do: Attend live concerts and events, and explore music history.

Packing List: Event tickets, a light jacket, and comfortable shoes for standing.

Best Time to Visit: Year-round, with outdoor shows in summer.

Fees: Ticket prices vary by event.

How to Get There: Accessible by car via Garden State Parkway, or by train to Asbury Park Station.

Closest Town for Accommodation: Stay at The Asbury Hotel, offering modern amenities and a rooftop bar just steps from The Stone Pony. Phone: +1 732-774-7100

GPS Coordinates: 40.2230° N, 74.0004° W

Interesting Facts: The Stone Pony opened in 1974 and has since become a cornerstone of Asbury Park's music scene, earning its place as a must-visit destination for music fans.

NATURAL WONDERS & OUTDOOR ADVENTURES

Cape May Beaches

Why You Should Visit: Cape May Beaches are some of the most beautiful and well-preserved in New Jersey.

Known for their soft sand and clean waters, these beaches offer a perfect getaway for relaxation and family fun. The Victorian charm of Cape May's historic district adds a unique touch, making it a delightful blend of beach and history. Whether you're sunbathing, swimming, or exploring nearby shops and restaurants, Cape May Beaches provide a classic seaside experience. **Website:** (https://www.capemay.com)

Location: Beach Ave, Cape May, NJ 08204, USA.

What to do: Sunbathing, swimming, and beachcombing. **Packing List:** Beachwear, sunscreen, and a beach chair or towel.

Best Time to Visit: Summer

Fees: Beach tags required during the summer; around $6 per day.

How to Get There: Accessible by car via Garden State Parkway, or by ferry from Lewes, Delaware.

Closest Town for Accommodation: Stay at Congress Hall, offering luxury accommodations with historic charm right by the beach. Phone: +1 609-884-8421

GPS Coordinates: 38.9351° N, 74.9060° W

Interesting Facts: Cape May is one of the oldest seaside resorts in the United States, with many of its Victorian homes now operating as bed and breakfasts.

Cape May National Wildlife Refuge

Why You Should Visit: Cape May National Wildlife Refuge is a haven for birdwatchers and nature lovers, offering over 11,000 acres of protected habitats. The refuge is a critical stopover for migratory birds, making it one of the best places on the East Coast to observe a wide variety of species. Visitors can explore scenic trails, enjoy wildlife viewing, and experience the tranquility of untouched nature.

Website: (https://www.fws.gov/refuge/cape_may)

Location: 12001 Pacific Ave, Wildwood Crest, NJ 08260

What to do: Birdwatching, hiking, and wildlife photography.

Packing List: Binoculars, a camera, and comfortable walking shoes.

Best Time to Visit: Spring and fall during bird migration seasons.

Fees: Free entry.

How to Get There: Accessible by car via Garden State Parkway, exit 10.

Closest Town for Accommodation: Stay at The Reeds at Shelter Haven, offering elegant accommodations with easy access to the refuge. Phone: +1 609-368-0100

GPS Coordinates: 39.0820° N, 74.8287° W

Interesting Facts: The refuge is part of the Atlantic Flyway, a major bird migration route, attracting birdwatchers from around the world.

Cape May Lighthouse

Why You Should Visit: The Cape May Lighthouse is a historic landmark offering stunning views of the Atlantic Ocean and Delaware Bay. Climbing the 199 steps to the top rewards you with a panoramic view that is well worth the effort. The lighthouse, built in 1859, is also rich in history, making it a must-visit for both history buffs and those who love scenic vistas.

Website: (https://www.capemaymac.org/cape-may-lighthouse)

Location: 215 Lighthouse Ave, Cape May Point, NJ 08212, USA.

What to do: Climb the lighthouse, explore the nature trails, and visit the nearby beach.

Packing List: Comfortable shoes, a camera, and water.

Best Time to Visit: Spring to fall for the best weather and views.

Fees: $12 for adults; discounts for seniors and children.

How to Get There: Accessible by car via Garden State Parkway, exit 0.

Closest Town for Accommodation: Stay at The Virginia Hotel, offering elegant accommodations just a short drive from the lighthouse. Phone: +1 609-884-5700

GPS Coordinates: 38.9339° N, 74.9607° W

Interesting Facts: The Cape May Lighthouse is still an active navigational aid and is one of the oldest continually operating lighthouses in the United States.

Ocean City

Why You Should Visit: Ocean City is known as "America's Greatest Family Resort," offering clean beaches, a lively boardwalk, and plenty of family-friendly activities. The town has a nostalgic charm, with its classic amusement parks, miniature golf courses, and old-fashioned ice cream parlors. Whether you're looking to relax on the beach or enjoy a fun-filled day with the family, Ocean City has something for everyone.

Website: (https://www.ocnj.us)

Location: Ocean City, NJ 08226, USA.

What to do: Enjoy the beach, walk the boardwalk, and visit amusement parks.

Packing List: Beachwear, sunscreen, and comfortable shoes.

Best Time to Visit: Summer for beach activities and boardwalk fun.

Fees: Beach tags required during the summer; around $5 per day.

How to Get There: Accessible by car via Garden State Parkway, exit 30.

Closest Town for Accommodation: Stay at The Flanders Hotel, offering oceanfront accommodations with historic charm. Phone: +1 609-399-1000

GPS Coordinates: 39.2768° N, 74.5746° W

Interesting Facts: Ocean City has been a dry town since its founding in 1879, meaning no alcohol is sold within city limits.

Delaware Bay Boat Tour

Why You Should Visit: A Delaware Bay Boat Tour offers a unique way to explore the natural beauty of New Jersey's coastline. The tours often focus on wildlife, including birdwatching and dolphin spotting, as well as the region's rich history. You'll enjoy stunning views of the bay, lighthouses, and maybe even a sunset over the water, making it a memorable experience for nature and adventure lovers alike.

Website: (https://www.capemaywhalewatcher.com)

Location: 1218 Wilson Dr, Cape May, NJ 08204, USA.

What to do: Birdwatching, dolphin spotting, and enjoying scenic views.

Packing List: A light jacket, sunscreen, and binoculars.

Best Time to Visit: Spring to fall for the best wildlife sightings and weather.

Fees: Prices vary; typically around $35-$50 per person.

How to Get There: Accessible by car via Garden State Parkway, exit 0.

Closest Town for Accommodation: Stay at The Grand Hotel, offering oceanfront rooms and easy access to the marina. Phone: +1 609-884-5611

GPS Coordinates: 38.9630° N, 74.9044° W

Interesting Facts: Delaware Bay is one of the most important bird migration sites in North America, particularly for shorebirds like the Red Knot.

Wetlands Institute in Stone Harbor

Why You Should Visit: The Wetlands Institute in Stone Harbor is a nature lover's paradise, dedicated to preserving coastal ecosystems and educating the public about their importance. The institute offers interactive exhibits, guided nature walks, and opportunities to observe wildlife in its natural habitat. It's a peaceful and educational experience, perfect for families and anyone interested in learning more about the environment.

Website: (https://www.wetlandsinstitute.org)

Location: 1075 Stone Harbor Blvd, Stone Harbor, NJ 08247, USA.

What to do: Explore nature trails, visit exhibits, and participate in educational programs.

Packing List: Comfortable shoes, a hat, and a camera.

Best Time to Visit: Spring and summer for guided tours and outdoor activities.

Fees: $8 for adults; discounts for seniors and children.

How to Get There: Accessible by car via Garden State Parkway, exit 10A.

Closest Town for Accommodation: Stay at The Reeds at Shelter Haven, offering luxury accommodations with beautiful views of the bay. Phone: +1 609-368-0100

GPS Coordinates: 39.0552° N, 74.7595° W

Interesting Facts: The Wetlands Institute is located on 6,000 acres of coastal salt marsh, providing critical habitat for a variety of bird species and other wildlife.

Wharton State Forest

Why You Should Visit: Wharton State Forest is the largest state forest in New Jersey, offering vast areas of pine woods, rivers, and historic sites to explore. It's an ideal destination for hiking, canoeing, and camping, with miles of trails and waterways to discover. The forest is also home to Batsto Village, a preserved 19th-century iron-making town, adding a touch of history to your outdoor adventure.

Website:(https://www.state.nj.us/dep/parksandforests/parks/wharton.html)

Location: 31 Batsto Rd, Hammonton, NJ 08037, USA.

What to do: Hiking, canoeing, and exploring historic Batsto Village.

Packing List: Hiking boots, a map, and camping gear.

Best Time to Visit: Spring to fall for outdoor activities.

Fees: Free entry; camping fees may apply.

How to Get There: Accessible by car via Route 206 or Route 542.

Closest Town for Accommodation: Stay at The Red Lion Inn & Suites in nearby Hammonton, offering comfortable rooms and easy access to Wharton State Forest. Phone: +1 609-561-5700

GPS Coordinates: 39.6435° N, 74.6887° W

Interesting Facts: Wharton State Forest is home to the famous Pine Barrens and the Batsto River, making it a prime spot for exploring New Jersey's natural and historical heritage.

Batsto Village

Why You Should Visit: Batsto Village is a preserved 19th-century iron-making town located within Wharton State Forest. The village offers a glimpse into New Jersey's industrial past, with historic buildings like the Batsto Mansion, a sawmill, and a blacksmith shop. Visitors can explore the village, take guided tours, and enjoy the surrounding natural beauty of the Pine Barrens.

Website:(https://www.state.nj.us/dep/parksandforests/histo ric/batstovillage.html)

Location: 31 Batsto Rd, Hammonton, NJ 08037, USA.

What to do: Explore historic buildings, take a guided tour, and enjoy nature walks.

Packing List: Comfortable walking shoes, a camera, and a water bottle.

Best Time to Visit: Spring to fall for the best weather and events.

Fees: Free entry; some tours may have a small fee.

How to Get There: Accessible by car via Route 542.

Closest Town for Accommodation: Stay at The Red Lion Inn & Suites in Hammonton, offering comfortable accommodations near Batsto Village. Phone: +1 609-561-5700

GPS Coordinates: 39.6413° N, 74.6465° W

Interesting Facts: Batsto Village was a major center of iron production in the 18th and 19th centuries, supplying materials for the American Revolution.

Ocean Drive in Cape May

Why You Should Visit: Ocean Drive in Cape May is a scenic coastal route that offers breathtaking views of the Atlantic Ocean, picturesque beaches, and charming seaside towns. The drive takes you through some of the most beautiful and historic areas of Cape May, making it perfect for a leisurely road trip. Along the way, you can stop at various attractions, including lighthouses, wildlife refuges, and quaint shops.

Website: (https://www.capemay.com)

Location: Ocean Drive, Cape May, NJ 08204, USA.

What to do: Scenic driving, beach stops, and exploring local attractions.

Packing List: Sunglasses, a camera, and a picnic basket for beach stops.

Best Time to Visit: Spring to fall for pleasant weather and clear views.

Fees: Free to drive; some attractions along the route may have entry fees.

How to Get There: Accessible by car via Garden State Parkway, exit 0.

Closest Town for Accommodation: Stay at Congress Hall, offering luxurious beachfront accommodations with historic charm in Cape May. Phone: +1 609-884-8421

GPS Coordinates: 38.9351° N, 74.9060° W

Interesting Facts: Ocean Drive offers access to some of Cape May's most iconic landmarks, including the Cape May Lighthouse and the historic Victorian district.

HISTORICAL & CULTURAL SITES

Cold Spring Village

Why You Should Visit: Cold Spring Village is a living history museum that brings the 1800s to life with costumed interpreters, historic buildings, and hands-on activities. You can explore over 25 restored buildings, including a blacksmith shop, schoolhouse, and general store. The village offers a unique glimpse into rural life in early America, making it a fun and educational experience for all ages.

Website: [Cold Spring Village](https://www.hcsv.org)
Location: 720 Route 9, Cape May, NJ 08204, USA.

What to do: Tour historic buildings, watch demonstrations, and participate in activities.

Packing List: Comfortable walking shoes, a camera, and weather-appropriate clothing.

Best Time to Visit: Summer for full programming and events.

Fees: $12 for adults; discounts for children and seniors.
How to Get There: Accessible by car via Garden State Parkway, exit 4A.

Closest Town for Accommodation: Stay at The Southern Mansion, offering luxurious accommodations in Cape May with historic charm. Phone: +1 609-884-7171

GPS Coordinates: 38.9740° N, 74.9091° W

Interesting Facts: The village is set on 30 acres and features over 30,000 artifacts from the 19thInterestin

African American Heritage Museum of Southern New Jersey

Why You Should Visit: The African American Heritage Museum of Southern New Jersey showcases the rich cultural history and contributions of African Americans in the region. The museum features an impressive collection of artifacts, art, and exhibits that tell the story of African American life from the early 20th century to today. It's a powerful and educational experience that highlights important aspects of American history.

Website: (https://aahmsnj.org)

Location: 661 Jackson Rd, Newtonville, NJ 08346, USA.

What to do: Explore exhibits on African American history and culture.

Packing List: Comfortable shoes and an interest in history.

Best Time to Visit: Year-round; check the website for special exhibits.

Fees: Free entry; donations appreciated.

How to Get There: Accessible by car via Route 40 or Route 54.

Closest Town for Accommodation: Stay at Tuscany House Hotel, offering comfortable accommodations near the museum in Egg Harbor City. Phone: +1 609-965-2111

GPS Coordinates: 39.5479° N, 74.8213° W

Interesting Facts: The museum also has a satellite location in Atlantic City, which focuses on local African American history.

Cape May County Park & Zoo

Why You Should Visit: Cape May County Park & Zoo is a family-friendly destination offering a free zoo with over 550 animals and a beautiful park with picnic areas, playgrounds, and walking trails. The zoo is known for its well-maintained habitats and diverse animal collection, including giraffes, lions, and red pandas. It's a great place for a day of outdoor fun and learning about wildlife.

Website: (https://www.cmczoo.com)

Location: 707 Route 9 North, Cape May Court House, NJ 08210, USA.

What to do: Visit the zoo, enjoy a picnic, and explore the park.

Packing List: Comfortable shoes, sunscreen, and a picnic blanket.

Best Time to Visit: Spring and summer for the best weather and active animals.

Fees: Free entry; donations encouraged.

How to Get There: Accessible by car via Garden State Parkway, exit 11.

Closest Town for Accommodation: Stay at The Reeds at Shelter Haven, offering luxurious rooms and great views in nearby Stone Harbor. Phone: +1 609-368-0100

GPS Coordinates: 39.0968° N, 74.8083° W

Interesting Facts: The zoo began as a small aviary in the 1970s and has since grown into one of the best zoos on the East Coast.

Wheaton Arts and Cultural Center

Why You Should Visit: Wheaton Arts and Cultural Center is a unique destination dedicated to the art of glassmaking and other crafts. Visitors can watch live glassblowing demonstrations, explore the Museum of American Glass, and shop for handcrafted items in the stores. The center also hosts special events, workshops, and exhibitions, making it a vibrant cultural hub in New Jersey.

Website: (https://www.wheatonarts.org)

Location: 1501 Glasstown Rd, Millville, NJ 08332, USA.

What to do: Watch glassblowing, visit the museum, and attend workshops.

Packing List: Comfortable shoes, a camera, and a shopping bag.

Best Time to Visit: Spring to fall for outdoor events and exhibitions.

Fees: $12 for adults; discounts for children and seniors.

How to Get There: Accessible by car via Route 55, exit 26.

Closest Town for Accommodation: Stay at Fairfield Inn & Suites by Marriott Millville, offering modern amenities and easy access to Wheaton Arts. Phone: +1 856-776-2400

GPS Coordinates: 39.3963° N, 75.0241° W

Interesting Facts: Wheaton Arts is home to the largest museum of glass in the United States, with over 7,000 pieces in its collection.

Lucy the Elephant

Why You Should Visit: Lucy the Elephant is a six-story elephant-shaped building located on the beach in Margate, New Jersey. Built in 1881, Lucy is a National Historic Landmark and one of the oldest roadside attractions in the United States. Visitors can tour the inside of Lucy, enjoy panoramic views from the howdah (the structure on Lucy's back), and learn about her fascinating history.

Website: (https://www.lucytheelephant.org)

Location: 9200 Atlantic Ave, Margate City, NJ 08402, USA.

What to do: Take a guided tour of Lucy and enjoy beach views.

Packing List: Camera, sunscreen, and comfortable shoes.

Best Time to Visit: Spring to fall for the best weather and open tours.

Fees: $8 for adults; discounts for children.

How to Get There: Accessible by car via Atlantic City Expressway or Route 9.

Closest Town for Accommodation: Stay at The Claridge - a Radisson Hotel, offering historic accommodations with ocean views in Atlantic City. Phone: +1 844-224-7386

GPS Coordinates: 39.3217° N, 74.5171° W

Interesting Facts: Lucy was originally built as a gimmick to attract potential real estate buyers to the area and has survived numerous hurricanes and the threat of demolition.

Cape May Historic Downtown

Why You Should Visit: Cape May Historic Downtown is known for its charming Victorian architecture, quaint shops, and historic landmarks. Walking through the streets feels like stepping back in time, with beautifully preserved buildings and a vibrant community atmosphere. The area is perfect for shopping, dining, and exploring the rich history of one of America's oldest seaside resorts.

Website: (https://www.capemay.com)

Location: Washington St, Cape May, NJ 08204, USA.

What to do: Explore Victorian architecture, shop, and dine in historic settings.

Packing List: Comfortable walking shoes, a camera, and a shopping bag.

Best Time to Visit: Spring to fall for pleasant weather and open shops.

Fees: Free to explore; costs vary by activity.

How to Get There: Accessible by car via Garden State Parkway, exit 0.

Closest Town for Accommodation: Stay at The Virginia Hotel, offering elegant accommodations in the heart of Cape May's historic district. Phone: +1 609-884-5700

GPS Coordinates: 38.9351° N, 74.9060° W

Interesting Facts: Cape May is home to the largest collection of Victorian-era buildings in the United States, earning it the nickname "The Nation's Oldest Seaside Resort."

Absecon Lighthouse

Why You Should Visit: The Absecon Lighthouse in Atlantic City is the tallest lighthouse in New Jersey and the third tallest in the United States. Visitors can climb the 228 steps to the top for stunning views of the Atlantic City skyline and the surrounding coastline. The lighthouse, built in 1857, also features a museum and keeper's house, offering a fascinating glimpse into maritime history. **Website:** (https://www.abseconlighthouse.org)

Location: 31 S Rhode Island Ave, Atlantic City, NJ 08401, USA.

What to do: Climb the lighthouse, visit the museum, and enjoy ocean views.

Packing List: Comfortable shoes, a camera, and water for the climb.

Best Time to Visit: Spring to fall for the best views and weather.

Fees: $10 for adults; discounts for seniors and children.

How to Get There: Accessible by car via Atlantic City Expressway or Route 30.

Closest Town for Accommodation: Stay at The Claridge - a Radisson Hotel, offering historic accommodations with ocean views near Atlantic City's main attractions. Phone: +1 844-224-7386

GPS Coordinates: 39.3643° N, 74.4153° W

Interesting Facts: Absecon Lighthouse was first lit in 1857 and remains one of the oldest lighthouses in the United States still open to the public.

Atlantic City Airshow

Why You Should Visit: The Atlantic City Airshow, also known as "Thunder Over the Boardwalk," is one of the largest and most thrilling airshows in the United States. Held annually over the Atlantic City beaches and boardwalk, the show features military and civilian aircraft performing stunning aerial maneuvers. It's a must-see event for aviation enthusiasts and families, offering a day of excitement with spectacular views. **Website:** www.boardwalkhall.com

Location: 2301 Boardwalk, Atlantic City, NJ 08401, USA.

What to do: Watch the airshow, explore the boardwalk, and enjoy the beach.

Packing List: Sunglasses, a hat, and a beach chair.

Best Time to Visit: August, when the airshow takes place.

Fees: Free to watch; VIP seating may have fees.

How to Get There: Accessible by car via Atlantic City Expressway or by train to Atlantic City Station.

Closest Town for Accommodation: Stay at Hard Rock Hotel & Casino Atlantic City, offering luxury accommodations with ocean views and easy access to the boardwalk. Phone: +1 609-449-1000

GPS Coordinates: 39.3556° N, 74.4266° W

Interesting Facts: The Atlantic City Airshow began in 2003 and has since grown into one of the most popular summer events on the East Coast, drawing hundreds of thousands of spectators each year.

Ocean City Historical Museum

Why You Should Visit: The Ocean City Historical Museum offers a fascinating look into the history of Ocean City, NJ, from its founding as a Christian seaside resort to its development into a popular family vacation destination. The museum features exhibits on local history, including antique furniture, vintage postcards, and artifacts from the city's early days. It's a great place to learn about the cultural and historical significance of this charming seaside town.

Website: (https://www.ocnjmuseum.org)

Location: 1735 Simpson Ave, Ocean City, NJ 08226, USA.

What to do: Explore exhibits on Ocean City's history and browse the gift shop.

Packing List: Comfortable shoes, a camera, and an interest in history.

Best Time to Visit: Year-round.

Fees: Free entry; donations appreciated.

How to Get There: Accessible by car via Garden State Parkway, exit 30.

Closest Town for Accommodation: Stay at The Flanders Hotel, offering oceanfront accommodations with historic charm in Ocean City. Phone: +1 609-399-1000

GPS Coordinates: 39.2707° N, 74.5984° W

Interesting Facts: Ocean City was founded in 1879 as a Christian seaside resort, and the museum preserves the city's unique heritage and traditions.

Cape May Trolley Tour

Why You Should Visit: The Cape May Trolley Tour offers a charming and informative way to explore the historic streets of Cape May, one of the oldest seaside resorts in the United States. The narrated tours provide insights into the town's Victorian architecture, rich history, and cultural landmarks. It's a relaxing way to see the best of Cape May while learning about its storied past. **Website:** (https://www.capemaymac.org)

Location: 1048 Washington St, Cape May, NJ 08204, USA.

What to do: Enjoy a guided trolley tour of Cape May's historic district.

Packing List: Comfortable clothing, a camera, and sunscreen.

Best Time to Visit: Spring to fall.

Fees: $15 for adults; discounts for children and seniors.

How to Get There: Accessible by car via Garden State Parkway, exit 0.

Closest Town for Accommodation: Stay at The Virginia Hotel, offering elegant accommodations and easy access to Cape May's attractions. Phone: +1 609-884-5700

GPS Coordinates: 38.9351° N, 74.9060° W

Interesting Facts: Cape May is designated as a National Historic Landmark District, and the trolley tours highlight the town's well-preserved Victorian-era buildings and landmarks.

URBAN ADVENTURES

Atlantic City Boardwalk

Why You Should Visit: The Atlantic City Boardwalk is one of the most iconic boardwalks in the United States, offering miles of entertainment, shops, and ocean views. It's a perfect place to enjoy a seaside stroll, visit casinos, and take in the lively atmosphere. With historic landmarks, delicious eateries, and a bustling beach scene, the boardwalk is a must-visit destination for both relaxation and excitement. **Website:** www.atlanticcitynj.com

Location: 2301 Boardwalk, Atlantic City, NJ 08401

What to do: Walk the boardwalk, shop, dine, and visit attractions.

Packing List: Comfortable walking shoes, sunscreen, and a camera.

Best Time to Visit: Summer for the best beach and boardwalk experience.

Fees: Free to explore; costs vary by activity.

How to Get There: Accessible by car via Atlantic City Expressway or by train to Atlantic City Station.

Closest Town for Accommodation: Stay at Hard Rock Hotel & Casino Atlantic City, offering luxury accommodations and easy access to the boardwalk. Phone: +1 609-449-1000

GPS Coordinates: 39.3556° N, 74.4266° W

Interesting Facts: The Atlantic City Boardwalk, established in 1870, was the first boardwalk in the United States and has inspired similar boardwalks worldwide.

Steel Pier in Atlantic City

Why You Should Visit: Steel Pier is an amusement park located on the Atlantic City Boardwalk, offering thrilling rides, carnival games, and family-friendly attractions. The pier extends 1,000 feet into the Atlantic Ocean, providing stunning views and a classic seaside amusement experience. From the iconic Ferris wheel to fun-filled arcade games, Steel Pier is perfect for a day of excitement by the sea.

Website: (https://www.steelpier.com)

Location: 1000 Boardwalk, Atlantic City, NJ 08401, USA.

What to do: Enjoy amusement rides, play arcade games, and dine at the pier.

Packing List: Comfortable clothes, sunscreen, and a camera.

Best Time to Visit: Summer for full access to rides and attractions.

Fees: Free to enter; ride tickets vary in price.

How to Get There: Accessible by car via Atlantic City Expressway or by train to Atlantic City Station.

Closest Town for Accommodation: Stay at Resorts Casino Hotel Atlantic City, offering comfortable accommodations right on the boardwalk. Phone: +1 609-340-6300

GPS Coordinates: 39.3575° N, 74.4233° W

Interesting Facts: Steel Pier first opened in 1898 and has been a popular destination for over a century, hosting famous acts like Frank Sinatra and Al Jolson.

Cape May Dolphin-Watching Cruise

Why You Should Visit: A Cape May Dolphin-Watching Cruise offers a unique opportunity to see dolphins in their natural habitat along the beautiful New Jersey coastline. The cruises are guided by knowledgeable experts who share interesting facts about marine life and the area's history. It's a relaxing and educational experience, perfect for nature lovers and families looking to enjoy a day on the water.

Website: (https://www.capemaywhalewatcher.com)

Location: 1218 Wilson Dr, Cape May, NJ 08204, USA.

What to do: Dolphin watching, enjoying scenic views, and learning about marine life.

Packing List: Sunglasses, sunscreen, and a camera.

Best Time to Visit: Spring to fall for the best chance to see dolphins.

Fees: Prices vary; typically around $35-$50 per person.

How to Get There: Accessible by car via Garden State Parkway, exit 0.

Closest Town for Accommodation: Stay at The Grand Hotel of Cape May, offering oceanfront rooms and easy access to the marina. Phone: +1 609-884-5611

GPS Coordinates: 38.9630° N, 74.9044° W

Interesting Facts: Cape May is one of the top locations on the East Coast for spotting bottlenose dolphins, thanks to its rich marine environment.

Atlantic City Nightlife

Why You Should Visit: Atlantic City is famous for its vibrant nightlife, offering a wide range of entertainment options, from high-energy nightclubs and bars to world-class casinos and live shows. Whether you're looking to dance the night away, try your luck at the slots, or enjoy a concert by top performers, Atlantic City has something for everyone. The city comes alive after dark, making it a prime destination for night owls.

Website: www.atlanticcitynj.com/explore/nightlife

Location: 2831 Boardwalk, Atlantic City, NJ 08401

What to do: Visit nightclubs, casinos, and live entertainment venues.

Packing List: Dressy attire, ID, and a wallet for the night out.

Best Time to Visit: Weekends for the most vibrant scene.

Fees: Varies by venue; cover charges may apply.

How to Get There: Accessible by car via Atlantic City Expressway or by train to Atlantic City Station.

Closest Town for Accommodation: Stay at Borgata Hotel Casino & Spa, offering luxury accommodations, a top-rated casino, and multiple nightlife options. Phone: +1 609-317-1000

GPS Coordinates: 39.3704° N, 74.4397° W

Interesting Facts: Atlantic City has been a hub for nightlife and entertainment since the early 20th century, with famous performers like Frank Sinatra and Beyoncé gracing its stages.

Ripley's Believe It or Not! Museum

Why You Should Visit: Ripley's Believe It or Not! Museum in Atlantic City is filled with oddities and curiosities from around the world. The museum features over 400 exhibits, including unusual artifacts, strange artworks, and interactive displays that fascinate visitors of all ages. It's a fun and quirky place to explore, making it a great stop for families and anyone interested in the bizarre and unusual.

Website: (https://www.ripleys.com/atlanticcity/)

Location: 1441 Boardwalk, Atlantic City, NJ 08401, USA.

What to do: Explore bizarre exhibits, interact with displays, and take fun photos.

Packing List: Comfortable shoes, a camera, and a sense of adventure.

Best Time to Visit: Year-round; rainy days for indoor fun.

Fees: $17 for adults; discounts for children and seniors.

How to Get There: Accessible by car via Atlantic City Expressway or by train to Atlantic City Station.

Closest Town for Accommodation: Stay at Caesars Atlantic City, offering luxury accommodations close to Ripley's and the boardwalk. Phone: +1 609-348-4411

GPS Coordinates: 39.3572° N, 74.4299° W

Interesting Facts: Ripley's Believe It or Not! was founded by Robert Ripley in 1918, and the Atlantic City location is one of the longest-standing Ripley's museums.

Tanger Outlets in Atlantic City

Why You Should Visit: Tanger Outlets in Atlantic City, also known as The Walk, is a premier shopping destination featuring over 100 brand-name stores offering discounted prices. Shoppers can find everything from fashion and accessories to home goods and electronics, all in a convenient outdoor setting. It's the perfect place to score deals and enjoy a day of retail therapy.

Website: (https://www.tangeroutlet.com/atlanticcity)

Location: 2014 Baltic Ave, Atlantic City, NJ 08401, USA.

What to do: Shop at brand-name outlets, dine at nearby restaurants, and enjoy discounts.

Packing List: Comfortable shoes, shopping bags, and a list of must-visit stores.

Best Time to Visit: Year-round; weekdays for smaller crowds.

Fees: Free to explore; costs vary by store.

How to Get There: Accessible by car via Atlantic City Expressway or by train to Atlantic City Station.

Closest Town for Accommodation: Stay at The Claridge - a Radisson Hotel, offering historic accommodations and easy access to shopping and entertainment. Phone: +1 844-224-7386

GPS Coordinates: 39.3632° N, 74.4373° W

Interesting Facts: Tanger Outlets in Atlantic City spans several city blocks, making it one of the largest outlet shopping areas in the region.

Cape May Restaurants

Why You Should Visit: Cape May is known for its culinary scene, offering a wide range of dining options from casual beachfront eateries to fine dining establishments. The town is especially famous for its seafood, with many restaurants serving fresh catches from the Atlantic Ocean. Whether you're in the mood for a romantic dinner or a family-friendly meal, Cape May's restaurants provide delicious food in charming settings. **Website:** (https://www.capemay.com/eat.html)

Location: 401 Washington Street, Cape May, NJ 08204, USA..

What to do: Dine at top-rated restaurants, try local seafood, and enjoy the historic ambiance.

Packing List: Casual to dressy attire depending on the restaurant, a camera for food photos, and an appetite for seafood.

Best Time to Visit: Year-round, but summer is ideal for outdoor dining.

Fees: Costs vary by restaurant.

How to Get There: Accessible by car via Garden State Parkway, exit 0.

Closest Town for Accommodation: Stay at The Virginia Hotel, offering elegant accommodations and an on-site restaurant in the heart of Cape May. Phone: +1 609-884-5700

GPS Coordinates: 38.9351° N, 74.9060° W

Interesting Facts: Cape May is home to some of the oldest continually operating restaurants in New Jersey, many of which are housed in historic Victorian buildings.

Jersey Shore Helicopter Tour

Why You Should Visit: A Jersey Shore Helicopter Tour offers a breathtaking aerial view of New Jersey's stunning coastline, including iconic landmarks like the Atlantic City skyline and the sandy beaches of Cape May. This thrilling experience gives you a new perspective on the Jersey Shore, making it an unforgettable adventure for both locals and visitors. Whether you're celebrating a special occasion or just looking for a unique way to see the shore, a helicopter tour is a must-do. **Website:** (https://www.heliny.com)

Location: Departure from Steel Pier, 1000 Boardwalk, Atlantic City, NJ 08401, USA.

What to do: Enjoy a scenic helicopter ride over the Jersey Shore.

Packing List: A camera for capturing aerial views, sunglasses, and comfortable clothing.

Best Time to Visit: Spring to fall for clear skies and the best views.

Fees: Prices vary; typically around $49-$99 per person.

How to Get There: Accessible by car via Atlantic City Expressway or by train to Atlantic City Station.

Closest Town for Accommodation: Stay at Ocean Casino Resort, offering luxurious accommodations with stunning ocean views in Atlantic City. Phone: +1 866-506-2326

GPS Coordinates: 39.3575° N, 74.4233° W

Interesting Facts: Helicopter tours provide a unique vantage point, allowing you to see the Jersey Shore's diverse landscapes from above, including its beaches, lighthouses, and boardwalks.

Adventure Aquarium in Camden

Why You Should Visit: Adventure Aquarium in Camden is one of the top aquariums in the United States, featuring a wide variety of marine life, including sharks, hippos, and sea turtles. The aquarium is known for its immersive exhibits, such as the Shark Tunnel and the Ocean Realm, where visitors can walk through tunnels surrounded by water and get up close with the animals. It's a fun and educational experience for families, making it a must-visit attraction in New Jersey. **Website:** (https://www.adventureaquarium.com)

Location: 1 Riverside Dr, Camden, NJ 08103, USA.

What to do: Explore marine exhibits, walk through the Shark Tunnel, and attend live shows.

Packing List: Comfortable shoes, a camera, and an interest in marine life.

Best Time to Visit: Year-round; weekdays for smaller crowds.

Fees: $31.99 for adults; discounts for children and seniors.

How to Get There: Accessible by car via I-676 or by ferry from Philadelphia.

Closest Town for Accommodation: Stay at Hilton Philadelphia at Penn's Landing, offering modern accommodations and easy access to both Camden and Philadelphia. Phone: +1 215-521-6500

GPS Coordinates: 39.9413° N, 75.1300° W

Interesting Facts: Adventure Aquarium is home to the only Great Hammerhead Shark on exhibit in the United States, making it a unique attraction for shark enthusiasts.

Borgata Event Center in Atlantic City

Why You Should Visit: The Borgata Event Center in Atlantic City is a premier venue that hosts a wide range of events, from concerts by top artists to comedy shows and boxing matches. Located within the luxurious Borgata Hotel Casino & Spa, the event center provides an upscale experience with excellent acoustics and comfortable seating. It's a top destination for entertainment in Atlantic City, offering something for everyone. **Website:** (https://www.theborgata.com)

Location: 1 Borgata Way, Atlantic City, NJ 08401, USA.

What to do: Attend concerts, comedy shows, and special events.

Packing List: Event tickets, comfortable attire, and ID for entry.

Best Time to Visit: Year-round, depending on the event schedule.

Fees: Ticket prices vary by event.

How to Get There: Accessible by car via Atlantic City Expressway or by train to Atlantic City Station.

Closest Town for Accommodation: Stay at Borgata Hotel Casino & Spa, offering luxurious rooms, a casino, and fine dining options, all within the same complex as the event center. Phone: +1 609-317-1000

GPS Coordinates: 39.3704° N, 74.4397° W

Interesting Facts: The Borgata Event Center has hosted numerous high-profile performers, including The Rolling Stones, Jay-Z, and Lady Gaga, making it one of the top entertainment venues in the region.

STATEWIDE EXPERIENCES

New Jersey State Fair

Why You Should Visit: The New Jersey State Fair is a beloved annual event celebrating the state's agricultural heritage with carnival rides, games, live entertainment, and delicious food. It's a fun-filled experience for all ages, featuring livestock shows, craft exhibits, and competitions that showcase the best of New Jersey. Whether you're there for the thrills, the food, or the culture, the fair is a must-visit tradition.

Website: (https://sussexcountyfairgrounds.org)

Location: 37 Plains Rd, Augusta, NJ 07822, USA.

What to do: Enjoy carnival rides, explore exhibits, and taste fair food.

Packing List: Comfortable shoes, sunscreen, and a camera.

Best Time to Visit: Early August during the fair's schedule.

Fees: General admission is around $14 for adults; discounts for children and seniors.

How to Get There: Accessible by car via Route 206.

Closest Town for Accommodation: Stay at Holiday Inn Express & Suites Newton, offering modern amenities and easy access to the fairgrounds. Phone: +1 973-940-8888

GPS Coordinates: 41.1374° N, 74.7104° W

Interesting Facts: The fair has been a tradition since 1821 and now attracts over 220,000 visitors each year, making it one of the largest fairs in the state.

Apple Picking at Orchards

Why You Should Visit: Apple picking at New Jersey's orchards is a cherished autumn activity that offers a chance to enjoy the outdoors and taste the freshest apples straight from the tree. Many orchards also offer hayrides, corn mazes, and farm markets, making it a perfect family outing. The experience of picking your own apples and enjoying the fall scenery is a delightful way to celebrate the season.

Website: (https://www.battlevieworchards.com)

Location: 472 County Road 513, Califon, NJ 07830, USA.

What to do: Pick apples, enjoy hayrides, and visit farm markets.

Packing List: Comfortable clothing, a basket, and sunscreen.

Best Time to Visit: September to October for peak apple season.

Fees: Entry is free; pay per pound of apples picked.

How to Get There: Accessible by car via Route 33.

Closest Town for Accommodation: Stay at Radisson Hotel Freehold, offering comfortable rooms and close proximity to orchards. Phone: +1 732-780-3400

GPS Coordinates: 40.2581° N, 74.3257° W

Interesting Facts: New Jersey is known as the Garden State for its rich agricultural heritage, and apple picking is one of the most popular fall activities.

Local Farm Markets

Why You Should Visit: Local farm markets in New Jersey offer a bounty of fresh produce, homemade goods, and artisan products directly from the state's farmers. Visiting a farm market is a great way to support local agriculture, taste seasonal fruits and vegetables, and find unique products like fresh jams, baked goods, and flowers. These markets provide a charming and authentic shopping experience.

Website: (https://www.collingswoodmarket.com)

Location: 713 N Atlantic Ave, Collingswood, NJ 08108, USA.

What to do: Shop for fresh produce, homemade goods, and artisanal products.

Packing List: Reusable shopping bags, comfortable shoes, and a list of what you need.

Best Time to Visit: Spring to fall for the freshest seasonal produce.

Fees: Free to enter; costs vary by vendor.

How to Get There: Accessible by car via Route 130.

Closest Town for Accommodation: Stay at Hilton Garden Inn Camden Waterfront Philadelphia, offering easy access to markets in the area. Phone: +1 856-858-1000

GPS Coordinates: 39.9178° N, 75.0730° W

Interesting Facts: Many of New Jersey's farm markets are part of the "Jersey Fresh" program, which promotes the sale of locally grown produce and goods.

Six Flags Great Adventure

Why You Should Visit: Six Flags Great Adventure in Jackson, New Jersey, is one of the largest and most popular amusement parks in the country. It offers thrilling roller coasters, family-friendly rides, and a variety of entertainment options. The park is also home to the Wild Safari, the largest drive-thru safari outside of Africa, where you can see exotic animals up close. It's a day of excitement and fun for all ages.

Website: (https://www.sixflags.com/greatadventure)

Location: 1 Six Flags Blvd, Jackson, NJ 08527, USA.

What to do: Ride roller coasters, visit the safari, and enjoy live shows.

Packing List: Comfortable shoes, sunscreen, and water.

Best Time to Visit: Summer for full access to rides and attractions.

Fees: Admission starts at around $50; parking fees apply.

How to Get There: Accessible by car via I-195.

Closest Town for Accommodation: Stay at Hampton Inn & Suites Robbinsville, offering comfortable accommodations and easy access to the park. Phone: +1 609-259-0300

GPS Coordinates: 40.1379° N, 74.4408° W

Interesting Facts: Six Flags Great Adventure is home to Kingda Ka, the tallest and second-fastest roller coaster in the world.

Cape May Seashore Lines Scenic Train Ride

Why You Should Visit: The Cape May Seashore Lines Scenic Train Ride offers a nostalgic journey through the picturesque landscapes of southern New Jersey. The train passes through historic towns, coastal marshes, and scenic countryside, providing a relaxing and scenic experience. It's a unique way to explore the area and enjoy a leisurely ride with family or friends.

Website: (http://www.capemayseashorelines.org)

Location: 31 Mill Rd, Woodbine, NJ 08270

What to do: Take a scenic train ride and enjoy the views.

Packing List: A camera, sunglasses, and a light jacket.

Best Time to Visit: Spring to fall for the best weather and views.

Fees: Tickets start at around $15 for adults.

How to Get There: Accessible by car via Garden State Parkway, exit 0.

Closest Town for Accommodation: Stay at The Virginia Hotel, offering elegant accommodations in Cape May with easy access to the train station. Phone: +1 609-884-5700

GPS Coordinates: 38.9358° N, 74.9097° W

Interesting Facts: The train route includes sections of the historic Pennsylvania-Reading Seashore Lines, which dates back to the 19th century.

New Jersey Vineyards Wine Tasting

Why You Should Visit: New Jersey's vineyards offer a charming escape into the world of wine, where you can sample locally produced wines and enjoy beautiful vineyard landscapes. The state is home to over 50 wineries, many of which offer tastings, tours, and events. Whether you're a wine enthusiast or just looking for a relaxing day out, visiting New Jersey's vineyards is a delightful experience.)

Location: Locations vary across the state; one popular vineyard is William Heritage Winery at 480 Mullica Hill Rd, Mullica Hill, NJ 08062, USA.

What to do: Enjoy wine tastings, vineyard tours, and events. **Packing List:** Comfortable clothing, a hat, and a designated driver.

Best Time to Visit: Spring to fall for the best vineyard experience.

Fees: Tasting fees vary; typically around $10-$15

How to Get There: Accessible by car; specific routes vary by vineyard.

Closest Town for Accommodation: Stay at The Inn at Salem Country Club, offering charming accommodations near many South Jersey vineyards. Phone: +1 856-935-7510

GPS Coordinates: 39.7320° N, 75.2267° W (for William Heritage Winery)

Interesting Facts: New Jersey's wine industry dates back to the colonial era, and today, the state is known for producing award-winning wines, particularly from European grape varieties.

PNC Bank Arts Center

Why You Should Visit: The PNC Bank Arts Center in Holmdel is one of New Jersey's premier outdoor concert venues, hosting top musical acts from a variety of genres. With its scenic setting and excellent acoustics, it's a fantastic place to enjoy live music under the stars. The venue has a capacity of over 17,000 and offers a mix of reserved seating and lawn areas, making it a great spot for both intimate and large-scale performances.

Location: 116 Garden State Pkwy, Holmdel, NJ 07733, USA.

What to do: Attend concerts and live performances.

Packing List: Event tickets, a light jacket or blanket for cooler evenings, and comfortable shoes.

Best Time to Visit: Summer and early fall for the outdoor concert season.

Fees: Ticket prices vary by event.

How to Get There: Accessible by car via Garden State Parkway, exit 116.

Closest Town for Accommodation: Stay at Courtyard by Marriott Lincroft Red Bank, offering modern amenities and easy access to the PNC Bank Arts Center. Phone: +1 732-530-5552

GPS Coordinates: 40.3919° N, 74.1725° W

Interesting Facts: The PNC Bank Arts Center was originally known as the Garden State Arts Center and opened in 1968. It has hosted legendary performances by artists like Bruce Springsteen, The Who, and Elton John.

Liberty State Park

Why You Should Visit: Liberty State Park in Jersey City offers stunning views of the Statue of Liberty, Ellis Island, and the Manhattan skyline. The park is a popular spot for picnicking, walking, and biking along its scenic paths. It also features the Liberty Science Center and a ferry service to the Statue of Liberty and Ellis Island. It's a peaceful escape with rich historical significance and beautiful landscapes.

Location: 1 Audrey Zapp Dr, Jersey City, NJ 07305, United States

What to do: Enjoy picnicking, walking, biking, and visiting the Liberty Science Center.

Packing List: Comfortable shoes, a camera, and picnic supplies.

Best Time to Visit: For nice weather and outdoor activities, spring through fall.

Fees: Free entry.

How to Get There: Accessible by car via I-78, or by public transportation from NYC.

Closest Town for Accommodation: Stay at Hyatt Regency Jersey City on the Hudson, offering luxurious waterfront accommodations with views of the Manhattan skyline. Phone: +1 201-469-1234

GPS Coordinates: 40.7033° N, 74.0551° W

Interesting Facts: Liberty State Park was dedicated in 1976 as part of the United States Bicentennial celebrations, and it is one of the few parks in the country with direct access to the Statue of Liberty.

Kittatinny Mountains

Why You Should Visit: The Kittatinny Mountains offer some of the best outdoor adventures in New Jersey, including hiking, camping, and wildlife watching. The range is part of the Appalachian Mountains and provides stunning views, particularly along the Appalachian Trail. The area is known for its natural beauty, with lush forests, clear streams, and abundant wildlife, making it a perfect escape for nature lovers.

Website: (https://www.nps.gov/dewa/index.htm)

Location: Kittatinny Mountain, Montague, NJ 07827

What to do: Hiking, camping, fishing, and wildlife watching.

Packing List: Hiking boots, camping gear, and a map.

Best Time to Visit: Spring to fall for hiking and outdoor activities.

Fees: Free entry; camping fees may apply.

How to Get There: Accessible by car via I-80 or Route 206.

Closest Town for Accommodation: Stay at The Appalachian Hotel at Mountain Creek, offering comfortable accommodations with easy access to hiking trails and outdoor activities. Phone: +1 973-827-2000

GPS Coordinates: 41.0812° N, 74.9252° W

Interesting Facts: The Kittatinny Mountains are home to the highest point in New Jersey, High Point, which reaches an elevation of 1,803 feet.

Classic New Jersey Diners

Why You Should Visit: New Jersey is known as the "Diner Capital of the World," with its classic diners offering a taste of American comfort food in a nostalgic setting. These diners, often open 24/7, serve everything from pancakes to burgers to milkshakes. Visiting a classic New Jersey diner is a must for experiencing the state's unique culinary culture and hospitality. Visit Tick Tock Diner.**Website:** (https://www.summitdiner.com)

Location: 281 Allwood Rd, Clifton, NJ 07012

What to do: Enjoy classic American diner food, from breakfast to late-night snacks.

Packing List: Casual attire and an appetite.

Best Time to Visit: Anytime; many diners are open 24/7.

Fees: Menu prices vary.

How to Get There: Accessible by car; locations vary across the state.

Closest Town for Accommodation: Stay at The Grand Summit Hotel, offering historic charm and close proximity to the Summit Diner and other local attractions. Phone: +1 908-273-3000

GPS Coordinates: 40.7162° N, 74.3570° W (for Summit Diner)

Interesting Facts: New Jersey is home to more diners than any other state, and the Summit Diner, established in 1929, is one of the oldest still in operation.

MAPS SECTION

Navigating with QR Codes

To elevate your travel experience, we've integrated a special QR code map that brings all key attractions into one user-friendly format.

Here's how you can maximize this feature:

1. **Effortless Scanning:**

   - Open your smartphone's camera app.

   - Point the camera at the QR code.

   - Tap the notification that appears to access the link.

2. **Interactive Exploration:** Upon scanning, you'll be directed to a dynamic digital map. This map allows you to:

   - Zoom in and out detailed views.

   - Click on for various attractions to access comprehensive information.

3. **Seamless Navigation:** Utilize the map to obtain directions and navigate to each destination. The map may also feature:

- Reviews from other travelers.

- Stunning photos to preview the sights.

- Some insider suggestions to make your trip even better

By leveraging this QR code map, you can effortlessly discover and reach must-see attractions. This tool ensures a smooth and enriching travel journey, making every moment of your exploration enjoyable and memorable.

Viewing the Interactive Map with the link

To help you navigate through the attractions with ease, we've provided an interactive map accessible via the link in this guide.

Below here's the link and how you can use it:

https://www.google.com/maps/d/edit?mid=1qEMKWgtcY YsWLTTy9mjp54tbOjTyB8A&usp=sharing

1. Access the Link: If you're reading this guide on a digital device, simply click on the link.

If you have a printed version, type the URL into the web browser of your smartphone or computer.

2. Explore the Interactive Map: The link will take you directly to our interactive map.

To obtain a better perspective of the region, you can zoom in and out.

Click on various attractions to get detailed information, including descriptions, photos, and reviews.

3. Navigate the Attractions: Use the map to plan your route and get directions to each attraction.

The interactive map will help you explore the area efficiently and ensure you don't miss any must-see spots

Thank you for choosing to explore New Jersey with this guidebook! I hope you found it exciting and informative as you discovered hidden gems, must-see attractions, and unique destinations across this beautiful state.

As a bonus, a map is included detailing all the attractions in this book. With GPS coordinates, best times to visit, accommodation options, and activity recommendations, this guide aims to make your New Jersey adventure smooth and enjoyable.

Now that you've explored New Jersey with this guide, your feedback would be greatly appreciated! It helps improve the guide and ensures future readers have the best experience possible.

Please take a moment to share your thoughts. What did you love? What could be better? Your insights are key to crafting even better guides in the future.

Thank you again for your support. I hope this guide helped you enjoy the best of New Jersey.

Safe travels!

CONCLUSION

As this guide comes to a close, it's clear that New Jersey is a state full of diverse and exciting experiences. From the breathtaking views in the Kittatinny Mountains to the relaxing shores of the Jersey coastline, New Jersey offers something unique at every turn. The rich history, vibrant culture, and natural beauty found throughout the state make it a place worth exploring time and time again.

This guide has highlighted some of the best places to visit, whether well-known attractions or hidden gems. But the true adventure begins when you start exploring for yourself. Use this book as a starting point, but don't hesitate to wander off the beaten path and discover new and unexpected places along the way.

New Jersey is a state that invites exploration and offers something for everyone, whether it's a quiet hike, a day filled with history, or simply enjoying the local flavors.

Hopefully, this guide has inspired a deeper appreciation for the Garden State and all it has to offer.

May your travels through New Jersey be full of discovery and unforgettable memories!

Made in the USA
Middletown, DE
04 December 2024

66133460R00071